Florida in the Civil War

Florida in the Civil War

A State in Turmoil

Sandra Friend

Twenty-First Century Books   Brookfield, Connecticut

To Rich, for helping me chart
a steady course toward my dreams.

Published by Twenty-First Century Books
A Division of The Millbrook Press, Inc.
2 Old New Milford Road
Brookfield, Connecticut 06804
www.millbrookpress.com

Library of Congress Cataloging-in-Publication Data

Friend, Sandra.
Florida in the Civil War : a state in turmoil / Sandra Friend.
p. cm.
Includes bibliographical references (p.) and index.
ISBN 0-7613-1973-5 (lib. bdg.)
1. Florida—History—Civil War, 1861-1865—Juvenile literature.
2. Florida—History—Civil War, 1861-1865—Social aspects—
Juvenile literature.3. United States—History—Civil War, 1861-
1865—Social aspects—Juvenile literature. [1. Florida—History—
Civil War, 1861-1865. 2. United States—History—Civil War,
1861-1865.] I. Title.
E502 .D69 2001   973.7'09759—dc21   00-069084

Acknowledgments

This project unfolded from a chance visit to Natural Bridge, where my interest in geology collided with my curiosity about history. It gathered momentum as I dug through research libraries for original diaries and letters, and visited historic sites around the state. Both Florida State Parks and the Bureau of Archeological Research provided valuable documentation for tracking down the many Civil War sites in Florida.

At the reenactment of the Battle of Olustee, many participants contributed to my education, including Bob McClendon of the 2nd Florida Cavalry, and Shorty Merritt, who filled me in on the *Maple Leaf* archeological project. After visiting the Civil War Soldiers Museum in Pensacola, I had a clearer picture of Pensacola's role in the war. The Museum of Florida History in Tallahassee enlightened me with its comprehensive Civil War exhibit,

as did the *Maple Leaf* exhibit at the Museum of Science and History in Jacksonville. The ranger at the Cedar Key State Museum pointed out some good local historical sites and resources, as did our knowledgeable guide at the Gamble Plantation. I talked with most of the rangers from Fort Clinch State Park, and with two of the cowmen from Lake Kissimmee State Park. At Fort Pickens, ranger David P. Odgen discussed history with me, and I managed to slip into Fort Barrancas late one evening for a feel of that garrison.

James Cusick and the staff at the P. K. Yonge Library of Florida History, Department of Special Collections, George A. Smathers Libraries, University of Florida made invaluable suggestions about original documents and out-of-print books to peruse. At the University of South Florida Library Special Collections Department, Paul

Camp and his staff pulled out some gems, including the little-known letters of George Colt and William Ellison. Charles A. Tingley, Library Manager, and the folks at the St. Augustine Historical Society Research Library have the serendipity of being housed in Frances Smith's home, and it was there I read her letters. Miriam Gan-Spalding and the staff at the Florida State Archives helped me feel comfortable during my many days in Tallahassee. At the library in the Museum of Southern History, Randy Karlin brought A. J. Neal's letters to my attention. Gail Shackleford provided support at the Pensacola Historical Society Research Center. Cornell University provided an important tool for my research: *The Making of America* Web site (http://library5.cornell.edu/moa/), which includes a full text search of the Official Records, more than ten thousand pages of reports by officers who participated in the Civil War.

Friends and family in Florida also contributed to my research efforts. Dale Allen, Deb Blick, Pete Durnell, Sylvia Dunham, William Hawkins, and Tom Saunders gave me leads to follow; Rich Evans, Mary Jane Gandee, and Linda Patton helped me chase some down. Thanks to Tom and Susan Schmidt, Gary and Millie Buffington, and Linda Patton for providing hospitality and lodging as I traveled to distant parts of the state. Thanks also to Mom for tirelessly clipping Civil War-related articles for my archives, and to Rich for serving as my proofreader and editor.

Contents

Preface · The Southern Frontier · 9

Chapter 1 · Independent Florida · 11

Chapter 2 · Pensacola, the Powder Keg · 16

Chapter 3 · Strategy on the Seas · 22

Chapter 4 · The Fight for Florida's Railroads · 27

Chapter 5 · The Politics of War · 32

Chapter 6 · Coastal Collapse · 37

Chapter 7 · River Raiders · 42

Chapter 8 · The Confederate Breadbasket · 48

Chapter 9 · A State Divided · 53

Chapter 10 · Bloody Olustee · 58

Chapter 11 · Florida's Final Stand · 64

Source Notes · 70

Recommended Resources · 76

Preface

The Southern Frontier

By 1860 Florida had spent only fifteen years under the American flag. Yet it boasted the nation's oldest European settlement—St. Augustine, founded by the Spanish in 1565. The British ruled Florida during the Revolutionary War, then Spain regained Florida under the treaty that ended the war. In 1821, Spain ceded Florida to the United States of America.

Most of Florida was a wilderness. But once it became a United States Territory, settlers moved in, especially plantation owners from Virginia and the Carolinas. U.S. troops fought to remove the Native Americans to the West. Speculators bought pine forests for lumber. Cotton, tobacco, and sugar plantations sprouted along the riverbanks. The economy boomed. Florida became the twenty-seventh state on March 3, 1845.

Then came the Civil War.

Early on Florida decided to secede from the Union. Nevertheless, Florida had a minor voice in the Confederacy. At the outbreak of the war, more than 140,000 people lived within its borders, a third of them slaves. Florida supplied more than 15,000 soldiers to the Confederate Army, but its own requests for defenses fell on deaf ears. Forced to scrounge for troops and ammunition, Florida struggled.

Union gunboats blockaded its coastline. Federal troops occupied many of its cities, taking control of all of Florida's strategic forts. Citizens were divided in their loyalties. Some had moved to Florida from northern states. Most owned small farms. Few wanted a war.

Governor John Milton feared that his state would be the first state of the Confederacy to collapse. In October 1861, he wrote to Confederate President Jefferson Davis, "The conquest of Florida . . . would . . . have a powerful influence upon foreign nations, an inspiring effect upon the minds of his [Abraham Lincoln's] troops, and of the people and Government of the United States, and form a basis for future operations."[1]

Yet Florida held on until the end. The capital at Tallahassee was the only Confederate capital east of the Mississippi to stay out of the hands of Union troops until after the war ended. Colonel John J. Dickison, a Florida commander who never lost a single battle, wrote, "There were thousands of men in our own proud little State whose brave hearts never faltered."[2]

This is the story of those men—and women—who struggled over the fate of Florida, the third state to join the Confederacy.

Chapter 1

Independent Florida

"We are threatened with the greatest calamity that can befall a nation. . . . Civil War stares us in the face, indeed it is war already and all though we feel that our cause is a righteous one, we know not how it is to end."[1]

As news of Florida's secession from the United States of America reached St. Augustine, Frances Smith wrote these words to her son, a major in the United States Army. Outside, the people of St. Augustine were celebrating "with firing of cannon & musketry, and much shouting."[2] Looking out her window, she could see Florida's new flag waving in the square. Several Florida militiamen walked into nearby Fort Marion and demanded the keys from the lone federal soldier watching over the ancient fortress. He asked them for a receipt.

Briefly, Florida was an independent nation before it joined the Confederate States of America. While some Floridians embraced freedom, others knew that war would change their lives forever. "I feel as if I wished I had not lived to see this day," wrote Mrs. Smith.[3]

Making the Break

During the presidential campaign of 1860, grumbling about the Republican Party spread across the South. Florida Governor Madison Starke Perry expected a war. After Abraham Lincoln won the election, Governor Perry told the Florida General Assembly that "The only hope that the Southern states have for domestic peace or for future respect or prosperity is dependent on their action

Black Confederates

In Florida, many slaves went to war. Blacks joined the Confederate Army for various reasons. Some were compelled to follow their masters into battle. Others felt close ties to their masters, and refused to allow them to go to war alone. They served as cooks and body servants, and might pick up a rifle if their master fell. Free blacks often joined the army as musicians. By April 1862, enough black musicians served in the Confederate Army that the Confederate Congress officially authorized their use, paying them the same as white musicians.[10]

now, and that action is, secession . . . ." He recommended "that a convention of the people be called at an early date to take such action as necessary."[4] Invitations went out for county leaders to meet in Tallahassee in January.

Governor Perry kept in close touch with Florida's two senators in Washington, D.C., David L. Yulee and Stephen R. Mallory. In December 1860, they pulled together strategic information, finding out the names, rank, and pay of army officers from Florida. Yulee asked the War Department for a list of all troops, arms, and ammunition in Florida. Suspicious, the secretary of war refused the request. Yulee urged the governor and others to seize the state's forts and arsenals. Governor Perry sent state militia to occupy the arsenal at Chattahoochee, Fort Marion in St. Augustine, Fort Clinch in Fernandina, and the Pensacola Naval Yard.

South Carolina seceded from the Union on December 20, 1860. Governor Perry offered his congratulations on December 24 saying, "Permit me to assure you, gentlemen, that gallant little Florida, will be the next to follow your wise and patriotic lead."[5]

In early January, convention delegates came to Tallahassee from as far away as Key West to debate whether Florida should secede. Of all of Florida's leaders, only former Territorial Governor Richard Keith Call bitterly opposed secession. He hoped "that no attempt will be made to declare Florida a Nation alien and foreign to the American people."[6]

While the delegates argued, Mississippi seceded on January 9. The next day, Florida's representatives voted to withdraw

Ordinance of Secession.

We, the People of the State of Florida in Convention assembled, do solemnly ordain, publish and declare: That the State of Florida hereby withdraws herself from the Confederacy of States existing under the name of the United States of America, and from the existing Government of said States: and that all political connection between her and the Government of said States ought to be and the same is hereby totally annulled, and said union of States dissolved: and the State of Florida is hereby declared a Sovereign and Independent Nation: and that all ordinances heretofore adopted in so far as they create or recognize said Union, are rescinded: and all laws or parts of laws in force in this State, in so far as they recognize or assent to said Union be and they are hereby repealed.

Done in open Convention, January 10th, A.D. 1861.

The Florida Ordinance of Secession

from the Union—a vote of sixty-two to seven. A ceremony in Tallahassee marked the signing of the secession document on January 11, making Florida a free nation. Call was not pleased. He warned, "You have opened the gates of Hell. . . ."[7]

Mallory and Yulee immediately resigned as United States senators. Yulee returned to Florida. Mallory headed for Richmond to join the new government.

In February, Governor Perry asked lawmakers to raise an official state militia. Militia units were mustered into Confederate service, starting with a regiment of West Florida volunteers who became the 1st Florida Infantry in April 1861. Volunteers were asked to enroll for six month's service. The Confederate Army and the state militia soon competed for men to join their forces.

Southern officers in the Union Army resigned their commissions and headed either to Richmond or Florida to await orders. Several Florida men played key roles in the Confederacy.

General Edmund Kirby-Smith

"I would rather shoulder a musket in the cause of the South than be Commander-in-Chief under Mr. Lincoln,"

General Edmund Kirby-Smith

said St. Augustine native Edmund Kirby-Smith.[8] A West Point graduate, he became a major in the Union Army. After Florida seceded, he waited until his replacement came to take over his command of Camp Colorado, in the Colorado Territory (now Coleman, Texas). Then he left for home.

As a leading Confederate general, Kirby-Smith fought at Bull Run and Manassas. Cut off from the rest of the Confederacy after the fall of Vicksburg, he commanded the Trans-Mississippi Department and was the last senior Confederate commander to surrender to Union forces.

William Wing Loring

Raised in St. Augustine, William Loring volunteered for the Florida state militia at the age of fourteen. He later worked for Senator Yulee, became a lawyer, and served as a state representative. In 1847 he joined the Union Army as a rifleman, and lost an arm in the fight for Mexico City. When Florida seceded, he resigned his command, saying, "I shall always hold myself ready to serve my State and the south, should the time come when my services will be useful to them."[9] He served as brigadier general of the Army of Northwest Virginia under Robert E. Lee, then led troops at

Vicksburg, Jackson, and Atlanta. After the war ended, Loring volunteered as a commander with the Egyptian Army.

Stephen R. Mallory

A native of Key West, Stephen Mallory served as the customs inspector for the port. After fighting in the Seminole Wars, he moved to Pensacola to marry his sweetheart. As a lawyer, he participated in local politics. He was elected to the U.S. Senate and worked on the Senate Naval Affairs Committee. As secretary of the navy, Mallory became the highest-ranking Floridian in the Confederate government.

Chapter 2

Pensacola, the Powder Keg

Under cover of darkness, several figures slipped toward Fort Barrancas, a formidable stone fortress protecting Pensacola. That evening, January 8, 1861, federal guards fired warning shots over the heads of these Florida militiamen. The Florida men did not return fire. Several hours later in Charleston, South Carolina, state militiamen fired on the merchant steamer *Star of the West*, which carried fresh federal troops to Fort Sumter.[1] War was imminent.

Hearing that Florida had seceded from the Union, federal commander Lieutenant Adam J. Slemmer swung into action. His men at Fort Barrancas destroyed their gunpowder and wrecked their cannons. They then crossed Pensacola Bay to take over Pensacola's largest fort, Fort Pickens, on Santa Rosa Island.

The commander of Florida's state forces, William Chase, had supervised the building of Fort Pickens. Not wanting to attack Fort Pickens with his small militia, he asked Slemmer to surrender. Slemmer refused. Unknown to Chase, the federal sloop of war *Brooklyn* lay at anchor in the Gulf of Mexico, waiting to drop off more troops.

News of the *Brooklyn's* intention reached Senator Mallory. "We hear the *Brooklyn* is coming with reinforcements for Fort Pickens," he informed U.S. officials. "We desire to keep the peace, and if the present status be preserved we will guarantee that no attack will be made upon it, but if reinforcements be attempted, resistance and a bloody conflict seem inevitable. . . . Our whole force—1700 strong—will regard it as a hostile act. Impress this upon the president,

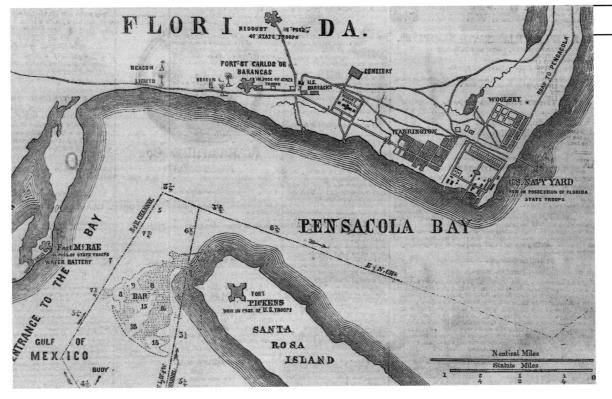

When President Lincoln was inaugurated on March 4, 1861, things changed. Lincoln's secretary of state, William Seward, suggested they "defend and reinforce all ports in the Gulf," and "put the island of Key West under martial law." Lincoln sent secret orders to tell the *Brooklyn* to land. In a choice between sending troops to take Fort Sumter or Fort Pickens,

and urge that the inevitable consequence of reinforcements under present circumstances is instant war. . . ."[2]

This letter became the basis of a "gentleman's agreement" between President James Buchanan and Senator Mallory. As long as the federal government did not send troops to help Lieutenant Slemmer, Florida's militia would not attack Fort Pickens.

he thought that "Fort Pickens would be . . . a more national and patriotic" choice.[3]

When the commander of the *Brooklyn* received Lincoln's orders, he refused to obey them. He knew he might start a war. Lincoln decided to redirect the troops to South Carolina, but the message didn't get through. Several ships filled with troops converged on Pensacola.

Confederate gunners at Fort Barrancas

On April 12, 1862, the day before the ships arrived at Pensacola, South Carolina militia fired on Fort Sumter. The Civil War had begun.

Watching and Waiting

Florida's militia held the vast Pensacola Navy Yard. They also occupied Fort Barrancas, a sturdy modern fortress built around an old Spanish fort, and Fort McRee, a smaller fort constructed on the sandy tip of Perdido Key. But Fort Pickens had the superior position. Taking over command from William Chase, General Braxton Bragg considered attacking Fort Pickens, but canceled his April 9 plans after word leaked out. Only three days later, troops from the *Brooklyn* "glided past those rebel batteries, which . . . could have blown their boats to fragments," giving Fort Pickens its needed reinforcements.[4]

As Bragg assembled Confederate regiments, Union forces massed on Santa Rosa Island, south of Pensacola. On April 16, Lieutenant Loomis Langdon wrote, "My company of 86 men are lying four or five miles off Ft. Pickens . . . while in the fort itself are 80 men. . . . The Secessionists are sequestering daily. They must have about

2,000 men. All eager for the fray, but I do not believe there will be any fighting."[5]

When President Davis came to inspect the troops in May, Bragg commanded roughly 10,000 men. "The Federals are infinitely superior in cleanliness and soldierly smartness," said Davis, but they "are not comparable in physique to the Southern volunteers."[6] Bragg focused on turning his volunteers into soldiers. Wrote recruit Len Griffin, "The military rule and discipline in camp is very rigorously enforced for sleeping on post—a chain and ball to one leg or 60 days imprisonment is considered and . . . some of the men will be shot for sleeping in post. . . ."[7]

After several attempts at landing near Confederate positions, Union forces attacked on September 14. The loss of the *Judah* provoked a response from General Bragg: "A party from Fort Pickens came to the Navy Yard, surprised our guard, and burnt the police schooner, the *Judah*, and wounded a few of our men and lost two of theirs."[8]

The Battle of Santa Rosa Island

"The night of the 9th of October was intensely dark. In the darkness 1500 rebels landed on the eastern end of

Confederate soldiers at Fort McRee, Pensacola, 1861. The lack of uniforms was not unusual.

Santa Rosa Island, and attacked Fort Pickens in the rear, hoping to catch it by surprise."[9]

Although they did not hold the island, the Confederates considered the battle a small victory. Roderick Shaw participated in the fight: "A party of 1000 men under Gen. Anderson and Col. Anderson . . . rushed the Camp of Wilson's Zouaves [the 6th New York Infantry] before they could get out of their tents the whole encampment was on

Wilson's Zouaves (the 6th New York Infantry) under attack by Confederate soldiers on Santa Rosa Island, October 9, 1861

fire. The Zouaves run like clever fellows & our men after them yelling at every step. By the time several of their batteries were spiked the regulars rushed out of the fort and tremendous firing was kept up for three hours. . . . "[10] Fourteen Union soldiers and eighteen Confederate soldiers died. The Confederate troops successfully burned the camp of Wilson's Zouaves, carrying away pistols, swords, and "several hundred dollars."[11]

Pensacola Abandoned

Occupying Fort Pickens, the Union Army had a superior offensive position. Soldiers could easily shoot cannonballs at the other forts, the Navy Yard, and even into the city. A barrage of fire tore down the walls of Fort McRee on November 22. Houses shook from the bombs. Dead fish floated to the surface of the bay. In January, a bombardment exploded the powder magazine at Fort McRee and damaged large portions of the Navy Yard.

Pensacola could only take so much pummeling. Under orders to join the Army of the Tennessee, General Bragg turned over command to Colonel Samuel Jones, ordering him to destroy and abandon Pensacola. On May 9, Confederate troops burned the city. "The public buildings, camp tents, and every other combustible thing from the navy yard to Ft. McCree were enveloped in a sheet of flames."[12] Residents piled onto railroad cars, carrying what they could. As the last train pulled out from Pensacola on May 12, the Confederate troops tore up the tracks behind it. Its destination: Greenville, Alabama.

A City in Exile

Although its buildings had been burned, the city of Pensacola continued to exist—in Alabama! The Florida state legislature approved the action. The mayor lived in Montgomery, and had regular meetings with his board of aldermen in Greenville. Alderman W.H. Judah received an exemption from service in the Confederate Army because he was an alderman.[13] The mayor charged Judah and Court Clerk Filo de la Rua with the "protection & safekeeping of the records and archives" of the city and the county.[14] After the war was over, the clerk dutifully retrieved the records. Seventeen packages of papers survived the war buried in large clay jars in the abandoned city.[15]

Chapter 3

Strategy on the Seas

Florida's biggest challenge during the Civil War was to outwit the Union blockade. Two fleets of ships sailed the coasts, patrolling heavily around major ports. Stephen Mallory assumed that a coastal blockade would be a major war strategy. He wanted to build smaller boats that could outrun and outgun the ponderous Union steamers. Writing to Jefferson Davis, he suggested building "small, shallow draft vessels suitably protected by iron plate, and with flexible ordinance."[1] He also enlisted blockade runners, men who made money by sneaking their boats past the Union ships. Florida's long coastline provided them a great chance of success.

Gateway to the Gulf

In 1846 the federal government had started to build two large masonry forts where the Atlantic Ocean and the Gulf of Mexico meet. Fort Zachary Taylor would protect Key West, an island city tied to the sea. Fort Thomas Jefferson, on the Dry Tortugas (a string of small islands west of Key West), would guard the entrance to the gulf.

When Florida seceded, Fort Taylor had a good stock of cannon and ammunition—but it had one open wall, facing the town. Only half of Fort Jefferson had been finished. Nervous after secession, U.S. Captain John M. Brannan

Fort Taylor

moved his federal soldiers into Fort Taylor. At Fort Jefferson, a group of fishermen landed and told U.S. Captain Montgomery C. Meigs about the state's secession. Federal troops landed to occupy the fort, and by January 23, 1861, the unfinished fort had 168 people living in it.[2] By February, the federal government firmly held both forts.

Key West: an Occupied Outpost

Because of its early occupation by federal troops, Florida's second-largest city became the only city in Florida under Union rule throughout the entire war. Some residents, like Robert Watson, headed north. "Owing to the political affairs of this country and the Federal troops having possession of this place," he said, "and as it is rather unsafe for a southern man to live here, I have determined to leave in disgust. . . ."[3] For those who stayed, sentiment over the occupation remained divided.

Some businessmen flew Confederate flags over their shops. By May, the occupying forces would no longer tolerate these shows of sympathy: "In no case must any other flag than our National one be permitted to fly over any Public Building. . . ."[4] On June 12, Colonel Harvey Brown reported "Key West as loyal, and that no future danger be apprehended of her disloyalty."[5]

Tropical diseases like cholera, yellow fever, and malaria ravaged the troops. They didn't have natural resistance against these diseases as the natives did. In September 1862, businessman Christian Boye warned his son to stay away: "The yellow fever is still here, amonge the troops and man of war sailors, they dy daily, how many is not known to the public. . . ."[6] Despite the deaths, fresh troops kept landing. The Union feared that England or France might take sides with the Confederate states, and the strategic naval position at Key West would be their primary target. Warned Rear Admiral Theodorus Bailey, commander of the Eastern Gulf Blockading Squadron, "The military importance of holding this gateway to the Gulf of Mexico can hardly be estimated."[7]

The Union Blockade

Bigger than any other fort in the Western Hemisphere, Fort Jefferson provided the Union a perfect base for the naval blockade. Enlistees signed up for blockade duty because of the extra pay. Whenever they captured a Confederate ship, the "prize" would be sold, and they would get part of the money. Louis Boyd had high hopes: "One of our Sailing Masters has about Ten Thousand Dollars coming to him, that is a very pretty little pile. . . ."[8] But shipboard life was tiresome. Assistant Surgeon Walter Scofield served aboard the U.S.S. *Sagamore* for three years. His diary describes day after day of sitting and waiting: "Musquitoes very plentiful in the evening, not a moments peace on deck or below. Slapping & killing them and finally retreating under the musquito bars. Got under head net and sweat it out with a sheet & cover-lid over me. Preferable to musquito bites, sweating is."[9] When they did get ashore, sailors found themselves "walking in bulrushes, wading in quagmire, drinking malar-

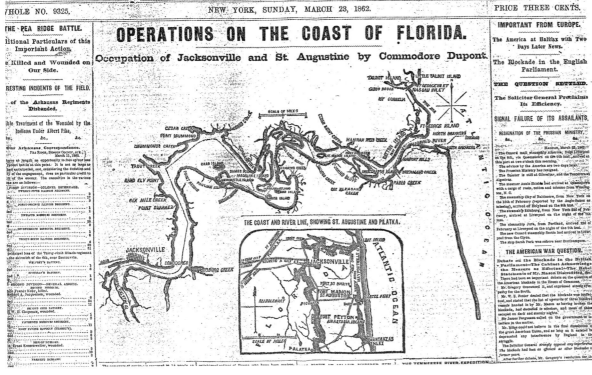

OPERATIONS ON THE COAST OF FLORIDA.

Occupation of Jacksonville and St. Augustine by Commodore Dupont.

THE COAST AND RIVER LINE, SHOWING ST. AUGUSTINE AND PILATKA.

A chart of Union Naval activity, 1862

ious water. . . . "[10] Even a dip in the sea had its dangers. "Attack of a shark in shallow water upon Horace Grey. . . . Water only three feet deep and yet the shark turned upon his side in order to bite. Lucky escape from his jaws."[11]

As Florida's troops thinned out in the spring of 1862, the blockading squadrons grew bolder. Instead of just chasing ships, they sent raiders inland to burn plantations, recruit slaves for the Union Army, and wreck salt-making operations. Aboard the U.S.S. *Albatross*, Louis Boyd participated in these frequent raids. At St. Andrew's Bay, he said, "we would leave the Ship about four O'clock in the morning, and proceed up the Bay until we would discover Smoke, for that is the only way that those pans [for salt making] can be found by a stranger, as soon as we would get near enough we would fire at them with a Small Cannon we have and such Skidaddling you never seen in your life, they would leave everything behind them, we went in Several of these Camps and found their Breakfast cooked and on the Table ready for eating which our boys would soon demolish, after rowing so early in the morning, we would then set about breaking up the pans & works."[12]

Destroying a saltworks. The ship on the horizon is the U.S.S. **Kingfisher**, a successful blockader that is also shown on page 56.

In early 1861, several Confederates disabled the light at Jupiter Inlet, carrying off the crucial lens pieces needed to keep the lighthouse working. They also destroyed the lenses of the lighthouse at Cape Florida. With these lighthouses darkened, many blockade runners risked the 191-mile (307-kilometer) journey from Nassau to the inlets between New Smyrna and Biscayne Bay.

The Union only caught nine blockade runners in 1861. But as the war wore on, they captured hundreds of small vessels in cat-and-mouse chases through inlets and tidal marshes. The captured ships went to auction, unless there was an immediate need to burn a ship to keep it out of Confederate hands. Crews were sent to prison or released on parole.

In a November 1862 speech, Governor John Milton said: "The blockade has cut off all intercourse with other countries, and for the present has rendered useless and valueless the staples by which our people have been able to raise money."[13] Although many blockade runners beat the blockade, the ships that were lost caused a serious drain on Florida's already stressed resources.

Beating the Blockade

Blockade runners carried Florida's cattle, cotton, and naval stores to the Caribbean to trade for arms, ammunition, and luxury items—everything from sugar and cigars to whiskey, rum, and silks. But how could the blockade runners beat the blockade? They used smaller boats—mostly sailboats, which sat higher in the water. These could easily glide over reefs and sandbars where the Union vessels couldn't go. They could sail into many inlets under the cover of night.

Chapter 4

The Fight for Florida's Railroads

The Union gunboat *Ottawa* closed in on the last train out of Fernandina as it crossed the enormous trestle to the mainland. Packed to bursting with frightened, fleeing civilians, the train raced against time.

"Boom!" An eleven-inch shell sliced through the last car. The ruined car sagged. A quick-thinking conductor unhitched the car, leaving it at the enemy's mercy. The engineer added more steam, and the rest of the train got away. The railroad's president, David Yulee, faced a grim situation. Stuck in that stranded last car, what could he do? He jumped. He hid until he could find a boat. That night, he paddled to the mainland under cover of darkness.[1]

Chartered in January 1853, the Florida Railroad took shape thanks to Yulee's business savvy and the construction crews of Joseph Finegan. By March 1861, it connected Fernandina, on Amelia Island near Jacksonville, and Cedar Keys, allowing goods to be transported overland from the Atlantic Ocean to the Gulf of Mexico. Yulee worried that his railroad would be a strategic war target. While still serving in the U.S. Senate, he wrote Finegan, ". . . the immediate important thing to be done is the occupation of the forts and arsenals in Florida. . . ."[2] This letter, found in Finegan's Fernandina home, implicated Yulee in treason against the U.S. government.

Cedar Keys Overrun

The unprotected western terminus of the Florida Railroad fell when the U.S.S. *Hatteras* steamed into Cedar Keys on January 15, 1862. The Confederate defense included only one officer and twenty-three men. The Confederate commander of Florida, Brigadier General James H. Trapier, had

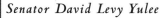
B-4411

ordered the remainder of the force to the other side of the state to protect Fernandina. Sailors from the *Hatteras* wrecked the cannon protecting the lighthouse on Sea

Horse Key. At Depot Key, they burned the railroad depot and seven freight cars, and pulled down telegraph wires. Yulee sent a train to evacuate the women and children. Fearing Fernandina would fall next, he sent his family to Margarita, their plantation near Homosassa.

Fernandina Falls

General Robert E. Lee had visited Fernandina in November. He wasn't impressed: "I have been down the coast to visit Amelia Island to examine the defences. They are poor indeed. I hope the enemy will be polite enough to wait for us."[3]

On March 3, 1862, as Union troops advanced, General Trapier gave the order to retreat and 1,500 Confederate soldiers moved out. George Dorman of the 1st Florida Battalion joined the march, reporting that "We received orders to spike the guns [make them unusable] and evacuate the place. I suppose they found out that the Yankees were going to land; any way we left the island that night, and all hands walked across a long railroad trestle in the dark, and luckily no one fell in."[4]

After Fernandina's last train escaped, the Union Army destroyed the trestle and occupied Fort Clinch. They were

Union troops marching through Fernandina

surprised to find ammunition left behind. With Fort Clinch, the Union Army could hold Fernandina against future attacks.

Baldwin, the Strategic Crossroad

The Florida Atlantic and Gulf Central Railroad connected Jacksonville with Tallahassee, ending just past Quincy. It met the Florida Railroad at Baldwin. Supplies headed south and food headed north, filtered through massive warehouses at the crossroad, so Confederate troops kept close watch on this important junction. The state's largest concentration of troops remained in Camp Finegan, just east of Baldwin.

In February 1864, six hundred men withdrew from Camp Finegan, unable to stop the advance of thousands of Union soldiers. The invaders burned the warehouses and damaged railroad cars on their way to what would be Florida's largest battle of the war.

Subsequent attacks cut off the supply routes to the railroad. Fortunately for Florida, the Union Army retreated from Baldwin to Jacksonville. By spring of 1865, concern remained that the Union might retake the crossroads. If they damaged the railroad "as to prevent the passage of cars . . . it will, in a measure, cut off South Florida from the rest of the Confederacy," said Major General Samuel Jones.[5] But Union attention remained elsewhere.

Fight for the Rails

After fleeing Fernandina, Yulee moved his office to Gainesville. Along with other central Floridians, he requested "General Trapier be removed for retreating from Fernandina." To "prevent the advance of the enemy into the interior of Florida," he suggested that the Confederate Army tear up the railroad and hide the rails in a safe place.[6] Governor Milton had a different idea. None of Florida's railroads connected to Georgia. Why not use Yulee's rails to build the missing link? The connection would speed up troop movements and shipments of Florida foodstuffs to the front lines.

Yulee refused, suing to prevent the rails from being taken. This infuriated the governor. Since many of Yulee's stockholders were northerners, the governor questioned Yulee's loyalty. "It cannot as it seems to us be reasonably presumed that those you represent can be entirely insensi-

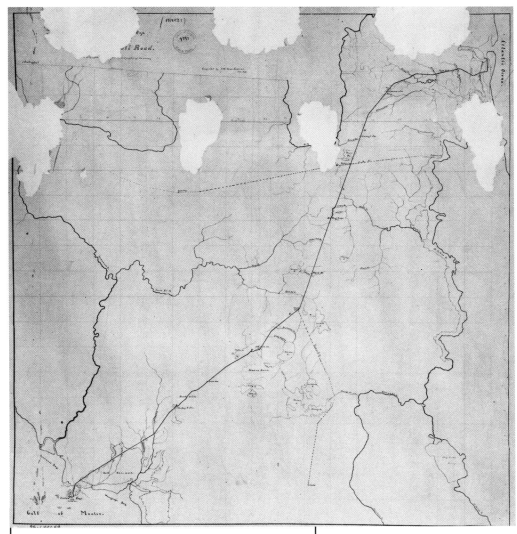

A sketched map of northeastern Florida showing
the Florida Railroad and proposed additions

ble to the general welfare of the State
. . . unless the Stockholders . . . would
prefer the subjugation of Florida to
the sale of iron at any price."[7]

By the spring of 1864, Major
Merriweather decided to ignore
Yulee's lawsuit. His troops ripped up
the rails from Fernandina to Baldwin,
using them to join the Florida Railroad at Live Oak to a rail line in Law-
ton, Georgia. But the connection came
too late. The new line didn't open
until March 1865.

Chapter 5

The Politics of War

When John Milton took over as Florida's governor in the fall of 1861, his number one job was to protect the citizens of his state. Florida had a serious lack of manpower. Confederate troops were being ordered to distant fronts to fight with the armies in Tennessee and Virginia. With these men gone, the state couldn't defend itself. Milton was afraid that Florida would be an easy target for the Union Army: "As it is, unable to conquer any other state, may not Florida claim their attention?"[1]

The Confederacy considered it a waste for soldiers to stay in Florida. The men spent most of their time sitting and waiting for something to happen. "Camp life very monotonous," wrote Joseph Dill Alison, a doctor stationed in Pensacola.[2] "The camp is on Perdido Bay, a half mile from the Gulf. The water is very bad, and the mosquitoes and flies awful. I do not think that there were less than 100

fleas on me. . . . "[3] At Robert Watson's encampment near Tampa, "it was so cold and damp that we could not sleep. Our beds consisted of a few palmettos [palms] spread on the ground, and a blanket spread over them."[4] He and his fellow volunteers did their laundry, built palmetto huts, played cards, and dug for oysters while waiting to be called to duty.

So the drain on manpower continued. As Milton complained to Stephen Mallory, "Florida seems to be considered of very little importance. . . ."[5]

For Family or Freedom?

Most of Florida's volunteers didn't care about the politics behind the war. They joined the army to protect their families and homes. Many worried that they would be

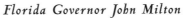

Florida Governor John Milton

Sergeant John "Alligator" Justice Ferguson enlisted
in the 2nd Florida Infantry in Jacksonville, July 13, 1863.
He lost his arm in the Battle of Chancellorsville,
Virginia, May 8, 1863, and was commissioned by General
Robert E. Lee to work in hospitals for the remainder of the war.

Private Walter Miles Parket, 1st Florida Cavalry

shipped out of state. Wrote recruit Washington Waters, "We are here on the coast and the Yankees' gunboats in site everyday, and the sandflies is worst than the Yankees. We are a fareing very bad here, and I fear that we will soon be sent west. . . . " [6]

When orders came in the spring of 1862 for Florida's men to head north to Tennessee, some resisted. The officers of the 1st Florida Cavalry wrote to the governor, "A few weeks ago we were perfectly willing to go anywhere ordered, but Sir, with the Enemy all around us our homes and families threatened we cannot think of leaving the State unless there is an Army left here sufficient to protect our families and interests; this we have communicated to the Major now commanding this portion of the regiment. We regret much to have been compelled to take this step, but death would be preferable to leaving our homes and families at the mercy of the Enemy."[7]

Some Floridians headed straight into battle at Chattanooga under the command of General Braxton Bragg. "Gen. Bragg says Fla. Soldiers stand what would almost kill ½ horse and ½ alligator," boasted Washington Ives, a member of the 4th Florida Infantry.[8] Other units were spread across Alabama, Georgia, Virginia, and the Carolinas. Eighteen of Florida's twenty-two Confederate units served outside of the state.[9] Experiencing harsh winters, disease, and disastrous battles far from home, many soldiers grew homesick. "You don't know how anxious the men are to be ordered to Florida again," said Ives. "If I ever get back to Florida no desire to travel will cause me to leave it."[10] All worried about their families. "The men are very uneasy about the news from home as the Yankees have already taken possession of many of their homes," wrote A. J. Neal of the Marion Light Artillery. "Our company was enlisted from almost every county in East Florida and I fear that communications with their homes will be cut off."[11]

On the Home Front

With the men off to fight, women oversaw farms and plantations. The Union blockade made supplies scarce. Frances Smith was "making experiments in converting sea water into salt in our kitchen, soap also is made in the house, & tallow candles!!"[12] At the governor's home, visiting tutor Catherine Hopley noted, "we had long contented ourselves without mustard, black pepper, and many other trifles . . . we often had no rice, even in a rice-growing State, no white sugar . . . no more tea. . . ."[13]

Many women contributed to the war effort by sewing and mending uniforms. Some created flags for the Florida regiments. A. J. Neal described the battle flag of the Marion Light Artillery as "an India Shawl of Mrs. Lewis . . . the ferule was a silver comb of Mrs. Capt. Dickison and the guilding is from the jewelry of several ladies in Marion County."[14] Sewing circles cropped up in almost every city to provide soldiers with clothing.

Other women helped blockade runners, acted as spies, or did what they could to confuse invading Union forces. In Ormond Beach, Mary Harper lived in a cabin with her small children, her eldest sons away in the army. When some Union soldiers came by with stolen cattle, they asked directions to St. Augustine. She directed them into a swamp! All of the cattle got away.[15]

Some trusted slaves supervised their master's holdings. "I am right in your house where you left me," wrote

William Ellison of Apalachicola to his master, a Confederate officer. "You need not give yourself any uneasiness about me for I intend to remain here until death or unless you move me away."[16]

War wasn't easy on separated families. "Cheer up, my darling, don't be sad," wrote Sallie Mickler to her husband Jacob, "your Dolly knows that nothing but your Country's cause would separate you from me while your life lasts . . . . Is this not enough to make us hate Yankees, but God says that we must not, how I pray that they may see their follies and go back to their own homes, so we can once more be together. . . . "[17]

Chapter 6

Coastal Collapse

"From Pensacola to St. Augustine, 1,400 miles [2,253 kilometers] and more, there was nothing approaching a fortification except the works at Key West and Tortugas, and those posts, the keys to the Gulf, were held by the enemy. . . . The Federal blockade was established at all the important ports, and the sight of the enemy's war vessels became a common occurrence to troops on the coast."[1]

To Governor Milton, protecting Florida's coastline seemed a daunting feat. But it had to be done. Unfortunately, General Trapier, commanding Florida's troops, did not agree. After his retreat from Fernandina, Florida's eastern coast was an easy target for a Union invasion.

The Occupation of St. Augustine

Federal troops landing in the nation's oldest city on March 11, 1862, found no resistance. The local militia, the St. Augustine Blues, had received orders on March 10 "to evacuate the place, spike the guns, divide the provisions among the citizens and march immediately to New Smyrna with the Artillery."[2] The unit was too small to repel a Union invasion. Instead, the Blues could help bring guns and ammunition inland from blockade runners landing in New Smyrna.

The mayor acted pragmatically by surrendering the city. Said U.S. Navy Commander C.R.P. Rogers, "I believe that there are many citizens who are earnestly attached to the Union, a large number who are silently opposed to it, and a still larger number who care very little about the matter. There is much violent and pestilent feeling among the women."[3] An incident where "several young ladies with their own fair hands cut down the flag staff on the Plaza . . . saying that the Stars & Stripes should not fly from that staff. . . ." added to the theatrics.[4] Union authorities warned

Artillery in Fort Marion with tents on the rampart

that such "exhibitions of Treason" would lead to arrests.[5] Frances Smith soon found herself removed from the city. As the seventy-seven-year-old mother of Confederate General Edmund Kirby-Smith, she was accused of passing "a rebel mail weekly into the interior." [6]

Union troops enjoyed St. Augustine. Soldiers dated local girls, scoured the bays for fresh oysters, went fishing, and played ball. Captain Blakley Mason wrote, "We have plenty to eat—drink and to wear . . . . We live well and the man that writes home that he don't is a—liar to speak plain about it."[7] By the fall of 1863, a convalescent camp opened for sick soldiers. When the 48th New York Infantry arrived, the bored soldiers created the "Olympic Theater" and put on plays featuring all-male casts.

Returning from New York, St. Augustine businessman George Colt noted the changes: "The Negroes here are all free and every one has left his former owner, I dint know of a single instance of one remaining with their master. A Negro school is in operation here for the instruction of the African children, and I see [the children] ran past me with slates, books & quite happy in their new life."[8]

But life in occupied St. Augustine grew painful for Confederate loyalists. In order to buy food, they had to take the Union loyalty oath. Nearly four hundred people refused to take the oath and were shipped to Jacksonville on a steamer. It wasn't allowed to land. When they returned home, they found their homes sacked and burned.

Jacksonville—The Wartime Pawn

On March 3, 1862, the Confederate troops retreating from Fernandina headed for Jacksonville. Expecting a Union invasion, the mayor issued an evacuation proclamation, but encouraged people to stay and continue to pursue their everyday business. Confused, the citizens panicked. Families packed their goods into wagons or onto boats, and headed into the interior.

By March 12, the Confederate troops were ordered to retreat. As they did, they burned eight sawmills, an iron foundry and workshop, a machine shop, and a gunboat under construction. They sank the blockade-running racing yacht *America* to prevent its capture. A mob looted and burned northern-owned businesses. Many stores along Bay Street were destroyed.[9]

As the Union Army landed, a welcoming committee surrendered the city. A public reception of Unionists urged

The Provo guardhouse in Jacksonville, Florida

a permanent occupation of Jacksonville. This horrified loyal Confederates. John Drysdale II wrote the governor, "Many of our respectable citizens both Male and Female have welcomed the enemy with Feastings, Union Speeches, and friendly Banners. Florida is disgraced. Abandoned."[10] Despite the positive reception, the soldiers withdrew, giving Unionists the option of leaving with them.

Union forces returned in October with a mission to stop blockade runners on the St. Johns River. After several successful raids, the troops retreated again to the barrier islands of South Carolina and Georgia, the southernmost strongholds of the Union Army's Department of the South.

In March 1863, another Union occupation force landed. Two regiments came from Maine, but the remainder of the soldiers, all volunteers, included runaway slaves. "It was the first time in the war (so far as I know) that white and black soldiers had served together on regular duty," wrote commanding officer Thomas Wentworth Higginson.[11] This occupation angered many. "Here were five hundred citizens, nearly all white, at the mercy of their former slaves," wrote Higginson. "To some of these whites it was the last crowning humiliation and they were, or professed to be, in perpetual fear. On the other hand, the most intelligent and lady-like woman I saw, the wife of a Rebel captain, rather surprised me by saying that it seemed pleasanter to have these men stationed there, whom they had known all their lives, and whom had generally borne a good character, than to be in the power of strangers."[12] Again, the occupying forces were ordered to leave. Upon retreat, the Union soldiers left nearly a third of downtown Jacksonville in ashes.

Finally, Union General Truman A. Seymour used Jacksonville as a base of operations for an attack into the heartland of Florida. Landing on February 7, 1864, he brought more than 5,500 men. On February 20, 1864, Confederate forces repulsed the Union invasion at Ocean Pond, near Lake City. The Union forces quickly retreated to Jacksonville. They set up makeshift hospitals, and put up fortifications to ward off an attack. Reinforcements swelled to almost 12,000 men. But no Confederate response came. Jacksonville remained in Union control for the remainder of the war.

Chapter 9

River Raiders

Rounding a bend in the narrows of the St. Johns River near Jacksonville, the *Harriet Weed* chugged along as it towed its prize, a captured Confederate schooner. Thirty-three men laughed and joked on the ship's decks as they watched the shoreline slip past.

Suddenly their world was "blown into fragments." An explosion threw the men into the trees and into the water, the ship collapsing around them. One man sailed 20 feet (6 meters) into the air. All injured, they struggled through the shallows to shore. They'd hit a Confederate torpedo!

"How are we to navigate these waters?" the skipper, nearly drowned and in shock, asked his commanding officer. "Take our chances," said the brigadier general, "with the pleasant feeling that at any moment we may find ourselves blown high in the air . . . ."[1]

Finding a defense of the coast impossible, Florida tried to defend its rivers. Union forces targeted the rivers for raids against plantations, carrying off foodstuffs for their troops. They actively freed slaves, and encouraged them to join the Union Army. Union gunboats on Florida's rivers were also free to capture and keep "prizes." But unlike their counterparts on the coastal blockade, they had more trouble with the deadliest weapon in the Confederate Navy—the torpedo.

Torpedoes: Explosive River Combat

A mainstay of the Confederate Navy, these floating powder kegs bobbed in the water, primed to explode on impact. In early 1862, Governor Milton was alerted to the usefulness of this weapon for Florida's fight. "I take the liberty of sending to you the plans of submarine batteries," writes his correspondent from Virginia, "which I think would be effectual in destroying the Gun Boats of the enemy, on most of our rivers in Florida, especially where the rivers are narrow."[2]

To be effective, a torpedo needed to hit its target near the waterline, causing the boat to sink quickly. Rather than depend on a ship hitting a bobbing torpedo at random, the Confederate Navy developed a version mounted on a long stick that could be pushed against its target. It would be delivered by a small, low-to-the-water armored boat— the *Viper*, designed specifically to attack the Union blockade of the Apalachicola River.[3]

Protecting the Apalachicola

The Apalachicola provided an important trade route for plantations in Georgia, Alabama, and Florida. For the Confederate Navy, it was the only route to the sea for ships built in the massive shipyard at Columbus, Georgia. It was important to keep this river open. But without manpower,

this was no easy task. In April 1862, Confederate troops abandoned the town of Apalachicola and moved upriver 50 miles (80 kilometers). Their job was to prevent Union gunboats from sailing up to the Chattahoochee River, the site of Florida's arsenal. The town of Apalachicola fell under the watchful eye of the Union blockading squadron.

In June 1862, Union Assistant Surgeon Walter Scofield expected the *Sagamore* to come under fire at the mouth of the Apalachicola: "They report the rebels preparing two iron clad gunboats to come down and attack us some dark night."[4] One such expedition left the Confederate sailors waiting for a week on St. George's Island because "the sea was smooth and the dipping of the oars in the phosphorescent water emitted a luminous light which shone brightly some distances beyond."[5] Even with the *Viper*, the Confederates were unsuccessful at routing the blockade.

Struggles on the St. Johns

After Jacksonville's first occupation by Union troops, it became obvious to them why the St. Johns River was important: It provided access deep into the heart of

A military post on the banks of the St. Johns River

Captain John Jackson Dickison of the 2nd Florida Cavalry

Central Florida. The Union's South Atlantic Blockading Squadron assigned a detachment of ships to patrol the St. Johns.

To counter Union raids, Florida's primary defense was Company H of the 2nd Florida Cavalry. Led by Captain John J. Dickison, this well-respected unit patrolled from Jacksonville to New Smyrna. Dickison's men never lost a skirmish, took prisoners against great odds, and returned thousands of dollars of property to landowners.

The company's most unusual fight occurred at Horse Landing on May 23, 1864, when they sank the steamer *Columbine*. Watching Union transports drop off troops at Palatka, the cavalry set up a position downriver: "Our guns were put in position at the wharf . . . the limbers and horses sent to the rear for safety, and our sharpshooters placed each man behind a cypress tree." They fired when the *Columbine* came within 60 yards (55 meters) of the company's position. "A double-charge of twelve-pound canister fire was opened upon it, with the result that the rudder chain was shot in two and the steering gear was helpless."[6] The *Columbine* could no longer maneuver: "She struck a sandbar; then a hot fight ensued."[7] Of the 148 men on the

*The capture of the **Columbine** on the St. Johns River*

boat, only 66 survived. More than a third were badly wounded.

While the destruction of the *Columbine* recharged Confederate spirits, torpedoes did much more damage to boats on the St. Johns than the cavalry could do. "I placed 12 torpedoes, containing each 70 pounds small-grade cannon powder, in the St John's River, near Mandarin Point, during Wednesday night, Mar 30," wrote Captain E. Pliny Bryan to General Pierre G.T. Beauregard. "Early Friday morning, April 1, I discovered a steamer, supposed to be

Preserving the Past

With the equipment of more than two thousand Union soldiers aboard, the sinking of the *Maple Leaf* was a considerable Confederate victory. For us today, it provides a peek into the past. Its cargo was perfectly preserved when the ship sank quickly into the deep mud of the St. Johns River. Instead of guns and cannons, the *Maple Leaf* is full of everyday items used in the 1860s—toothbrushes, pencils, chess pieces, flutes, and shoes. An exhibit at the Museum of Science and History in Jacksonville shows some of the items that divers have recovered from the ship.

the *Maple Leaf*, sunk off Mandarin Point. On account of the wind I could not board her until Saturday morning, April 2, at which time she was fired in three places and burnt. The water was about 2 feet deep on the upper cabin deck. But few things could have been saved by the enemy, as the vessel must have sunk in a few moments. She apparently was greatly damaged by the explosion. A few mattresses, sofas, wash-bowls, and other unimportant articles were left in the upper cabin. From her length, width, size, and general appearance I suppose her to be a first-class vessel."[8]

Confederate torpedoes sank four large Union troop transport ships in the St. Johns. Using torpedoes, the Confederates had a fighting chance against the Union raiders that plagued Florida's rivers.

Chapter 8

The Confederate Breadbasket

By the fall of 1862, Florida's role in the Confederacy shifted. It had something the Confederate Army needed even more than troops—food. Soon, the Confederate commissary wanted to "take steps to obtain some of the large supplies," most important of which was "enough beef-cattle in Florida to supply our entire forces for two years."[1]

The Union Army became aware of this change as well. "The whole dependence of the Confederate government to feed their army now rests on this State," wrote Union Navy Commander Maxwell Woodhull after a trip up the St. Johns. "I have it from reliable sources that its agents are all over the state buying up all the cattle obtainable. . . . The greatest blow of this war would be the entire destruction of the sugar crop and the small salt-works along the shore on the coast of this State."[2]

Salt of the Earth

In these days before refrigeration, salt was crucial for preserving meat. Leather-making also required salt, and the troops needed boots. Salt also figured in wartime commerce with foreign nations. A boatload of salt could be swapped for rifles and ammunition.

Florida's long coastline and hundreds of miles of salt marshes made it easy to make salt by evaporating Gulf water. Thousands of small Confederate salt works flourished, with a heavy concentration in the hard-to-reach bayous between Cedar Keys and St. Andrew's Bay.[3] The profit was enormous. The price of salt rose from $1 a bushel in 1861 to $50 a bushel in late 1864. One operation near St. Marks was making $60,000 worth of salt every day![4]

Water would be scooped from the tidal marshes into iron kettles, and a fire built under each kettle. As the water boiled away, it left a thick brown crust "nicely crystallized in cubical crystals" on the boiler's iron walls.[5] Scraped out and set to dry, salt would turn white after a few days in the sun. Only white salt could be used for preserving meat. Barrels of salt went by mule and horse over the tidal flats to waiting boats, whose captains tried to beat the Union blockade.

Plantation Bounty

Large plantations tended by slaves flourished along Florida's rivers. David Yulee's plantation on the Homosassa River produced as much as 185,000 pounds (83,914 kilograms) of sugar and 90,000 pounds (40,823 kilograms) of cotton every year.[6] In addition to sugarcane and cotton, tobacco, corn, rice, potatoes, and peas were major crops.

If a farmer wanted to avoid being drafted into the army, he could sign a contract to deliver specific amounts of food to the commissary. Acting as brokers for the Con-

Banana plantation along the Indian River, 1860

Naval Stores

Wooden sailing ships relied on the sap of pine trees for naval stores—tar, pitch, rosin, and turpentine. These products sealed and protected the wood from the harsh effects of salt water. Florida had a booming turpentine industry when the Civil War broke out. Turpentine factories became strategic targets. The Union blockade seized or burned any naval stores they could find.

Lumber, too, was an important resource. "The best peg on which to hang an expedition in the Department of the South, in those days, was the promise of lumber," wrote Union Colonel Thomas Wentworth Higginson. "Dwelling in the very land of Southern pine, the Department authorities had to send north for it, at great expense."[17] The Union troops used lumber to repair their boats and to build floors for their tents.

federate States of America, commissary officers purchased food and finished goods for the troops. Recognizing the value of Florida's crops and livestock, the Florida legislature passed an act in 1861 making export of meat, salt, corn, or "other provisions" illegal. No other state in the Confederacy had such a law.[7] Still, Floridians sold their goods to whomever they could. Yulee sold sugar to the City of Savannah.[8] James McKay sold cows to Cuba for $30 per cow in Spanish gold coins, when the Confederates only paid $8 per cow in Confederate dollars. South Florida residents drove cattle to Boca Raton in exchange for goods from blockade runners.[9] But as the war went on and supplies dwindled, the government forced citizens to sell to the commissary and "impressed," or seized, their crops for the army.

Home on the Range

After the surrender of Vicksburg, Mississippi, to Union General Ulysses S. Grant on July 4, 1863, Confederate supplies of Texas beef were cut off. The Confederate government finally turned its attention to Florida's biggest asset to the war effort—beef.

In 1861, cattle baron Jacob "King of the Crackers" Summerlin enlisted as the commissary sergeant for Tampa's militia. He bought and shipped cattle north for the Confederate Army. It would take a month to round up and drive a herd of cattle, following old trails from Fort Meade through Brooksville. A rest stop at Paynes Prairie allowed the cattle to fatten up before reaching Baldwin. The cowmen drove six hundred head of cattle to the railroad every week.[10]

It took very little effort to raise cattle in Florida. Cattle roamed freely over hundreds of thousands of acres of empty land from Tampa south, on the prairies around Lake Okeechobee, and along many rivers— the Myakka, the Caloosahatchee, the Peace, and the Kissimmee. When it came time to bring the cattle to market, Florida cowmen, called "crackers" for the sound of their bullwhips over the herd, rounded up the animals and drove them toward a port.

Because of the cattle trade, a small Confederate garrison watched over Tampa. Twice the Union fleet asked for the city's surrender. On June 30, 1862, Captain J.W. Pearson told the blockade that his men "did not understand the meaning of the word surrender."[11] The Union ships shelled the town that evening, hitting the courthouse and a private home. But without a landing force to back them up, there was no point to the battle, so they withdrew.

Florida's Cow Cavalry

After Summerlin resigned, James McKay Sr. became commissary for South Florida. McKay corresponded with Major Pleasants Woodson White, the chief commissary of Florida. White's greatest concern was getting Florida beef to starving troops.

"We are almost entirely dependent on Florida," wrote Chief Commissary Major H.C. Guerin of South Carolina.[12] After a bombardment of requests, Major White composed a circular insisting that Floridians must feed the "vast armies, whether producers will sell to us or not."[13] McKay received this confidential circular, as did many other prominent men around the state. But someone passed it around. It showed up on trees, fence posts, and crossroads. Union officers saw it, and changed their strategy. Their raids would target cattle.

McKay persuaded the Confederate Army to raise a special detachment to protect the cattle drives. In October 1863, "60 men of Dickisons Cavalry . . ." arrived in Tampa to form the Cattle Guard Battalion.[14] During 1864, they accompanied cattle drives north. They patrolled from Lake Okechobee to Lafayette County, and opened trade with the Seminoles. Confederate General Lucius B. Northup commended them for "operating in a country infested with traitors and deserters," noting that they "checked desertions and restored the confidence of the people."[15]

In February 1865, two hundred Confederate cavalrymen and soldiers traveled overland to Fort Myers to attack the Union garrison responsible for the cattle raids. The garrison refused to surrender. A few Confederates opened fire, but their commander stopped them. Women and children were inside the fort. Wrote First Sergeant Thomas Ellis, "We thought sure we would attack, but not so . . . I asked the Major why he did not make the attempt, and he did not think a good General would take the risk of having his men slaughtered."[16] This skirmish was the southernmost engagement of the Civil War.

Chapter 9

A State Divided

By 1863, Florida was in serious turmoil. Most of the coastal cities were under Union rule. The Confederate States of America wasn't doing well in the war. Rather than rely on volunteers, the army started to conscript soldiers. Governor Milton knew this would cause trouble. When the Confederate Army drafted men, it sent them north to serve on the battlefields. If a man joined the Union Army in Florida, he'd be less likely to get killed. Union volunteers from Florida stayed in Florida. Thousands of Florida men deserted the Confederate Army. They hid in the swamps or sought Union protection.

As conditions worsened, people spoke openly against the Confederate government. Milton noted that "a very large proportion, if not a majority of the citizens left in West FL are represented to be disloyal—at all events advocate reconstruction and have threatened to raise the U.S. flag even in Marianna," his hometown.[1] Even loyal soldiers complained. In March 1863, Robert Watson wrote, "I will say here that Confederate soldiers are treated like dogs everywhere I have been since I left Tampa. They are not allowed on half the rations that the army regulations call for . . . . Men are kept in hospitals when the doctors know that they will never recover . . . yet they will not give them the furloughs to go home but keep them here to die."[2]

A War-Weary Populace

By late 1864, Florida's food supplies had dwindled to dangerous levels. The Confederate commissary started to "impress," or seize, food from protesting farmers. Reverend John R. Richards pleaded with Governor Milton to intervene. "There are soldiers' families in my neighborhood that the last head of cattle have been taken from them and drove off . . . " Judge P.G. Wall complained to the governor.[3] "If we have arrived at the point where it has become actually necessary to impress all the cows in the country, then I say, God help us, for starvation must be inevitable."[4]

Floridians fighting on distant battlefields felt forgotten by the folks at home. From Chattanooga, Washington Ives wrote, "I wish the people of Florida would make up a collection of little things such as black pepper, salt, sugar, soap, ect To send the boys out here, our regiment is nearly destitude of clothing, shoes, hats, and pants. . . . "[5]

Desperate Deserters

Deserters from Georgia and Alabama came into Florida to hide from their regiments or to try to reach the safety of the Union blockade. In January 1863, Ethelred Philips warned that "the country for fifty miles between here [Marianna] and the Gulf is infested with hundreds of deserters in communication with the enemy. A few nights

Black Union infantryman

54

ago 44 deserted from one company and fifteen the night before. They had not been paid since June and their families were suffering from want of food. Everybody is tired of this war."[6] In February 1864, a group of nearly a hundred deserters tried to ambush the governor on his way home to Marianna. But a loyal Confederate citizen warned Milton in time.

Many deserters became outlaws, attacking travelers. A wagon train headed from Gainesville to Tampa in February was ambushed and captured by deserters at the Hillsborough River.[7] In Polk County, Joel Watkins received a letter from his sister, who was "truly thankful you all have escaped so well from the marauding bands which have infested Southern Florida."[8]

James McKay reported numerous desertions in Tampa. By May 3, 1864, he warned that South Florida would fall: "The Traitors and deserters now are getting so strong . . . I am at a loss as I am placed betwixt two fires the enemy being south, West & East, and nothing saves us but the forbearance of the enemy. . . . "[9] That very day, a party of eighty black Union soldiers landed in Tampa. They captured Fort Brooke and, at the hotel, "arrested some of the leading citizens."[10]

Union Army Recruitment

Union soldiers actively recruited free blacks and runaway slaves for the U.S. Colored Troops. "Col. Beard is recruiting among the blacks for a Regiment which are to be mustered into the service of the Government at once," wrote George Colt from St. Augustine in December 1862. "Rumor says they are to garrison this and other places on the Coast."[11] Special efforts were later made to send recruiters into the interior. After the Confederates shot a black prisoner who tried to escape, S.M. Hankins discovered "underneath his old rags, we found he had a full Yankee uniform with corporal stripes on them, supposed to be a recruiting officer sent out from Cedar Keys to Negro plantations."[12] By the end of the war, black soldiers made up much of the Union occupation force in Florida. Nearly one tenth of Florida's black adult male population joined the Union Army.[13]

Union forces also recruited dissatisfied white Floridians to serve in the Union Army. Brigadier General Daniel P. Woodbury sent a Union officer to "camp on one of the islands in Charlotte Harbor, and enlist as many men as possible."[14] Fort Myers filled with Union sympathizers. In

African Americans sail to escape slavery. They hope to be picked up by the U.S.S. Kingfisher, *a Union blockade ship.*

Pensacola, General Alexander Asboth organized Confederate deserters into a volunteer regiment, the 1st Florida Cavalry (Union). The regiment regularly invaded towns in Florida and Alabama, carrying off "negroes, horses, mules, oxen, turkeys, chickens, corn, meat, and everything they could find to eat."[15] Their most infamous raid took place on September 27, 1864, in the governor's hometown of Marianna.

Attack on Marianna

Marianna's primary defense was the Greenwood Home Guard, made up of boys too young to be drafted and men older than fifty. When the Union cavalry charged, the "body of militia, who were concealed in houses, churches, and stores, opened a furious fire."[16] Nearly twenty-two Union soldiers fell.

With no help coming from the few Confederate cavalrymen in the town, the Home Guard drew back. Some of them took refuge in the Episcopal Church. According to Armstrong Purdee, a freed slave, "Very soon it was said . . . that the General [Asboth] was shot. Orders were given to fire the church . . . it blazed up. Men were shot down as they came out of the building."[17]

Four men died inside the burning building. The Union troops went on to loot the town and carry off prisoners, including a fourteen-year-old boy who fought against them. The spirit of the governor's hometown was broken.

Chapter 10

Bloody Olustee

The palmetto thicket goes on in every direction, broken only by tall slender pines. There are no sounds but the call of a dove, the roar of the wind, the dried fronds of palmettos rattling. As Winston Stephens of the 2nd Florida Cavalry walks through the aftermath of Florida's bloodiest battle, the crickets stop chirping.

"I went over the battleground this morning on my way to camp and never in all my life have I seen such a distressing sight, some men with their legs carried off others with their brains out and mangled in every conceivable way and then our men commenced stripping them of their clothing and left their bodies naked."

It's a horrifying morning for Stephens, even though the Confederate Army won the battle. "I never want to see another battle or go on the field after it is over."[1]

A Fateful Decision

In early 1864, Major General Quincy Gillmore, the commander of the Union Army's Department of the South, decided to expand Union operations in Florida. Among his objectives, he planned: "To procure an outlet for cotton, lumber, timber, turpentine, and the other products of the State . . . to cut off one of the enemy's sources of commissary supplies. . . . To obtain recruits for my colored regiments . . . To inaugurate measures for the speedy restoration of Florida to her allegiance. . . . "[2]

On February 7, Union troops under General Truman A. Seymour landed in Jacksonville. President Lincoln's personal secretary, John Hay, joined them. If he could get at least 7,800 Floridians to sign an oath of allegiance to the

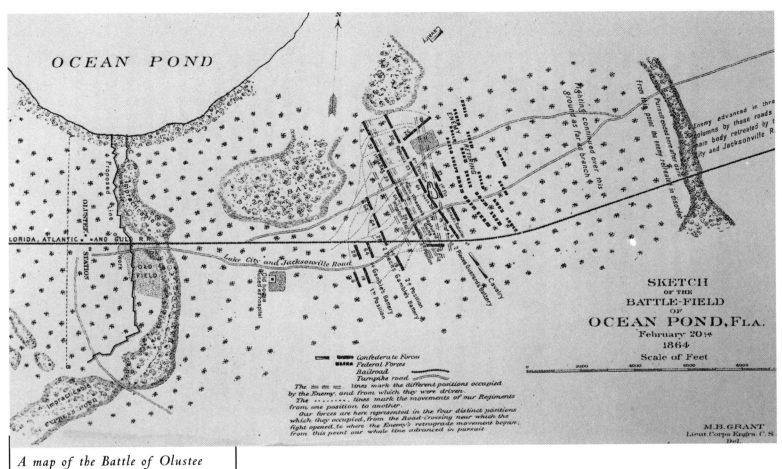

OCEAN POND

SKETCH
OF THE
BATTLE-FIELD
OF
OCEAN POND, FLA.
February 20th
1864
Scale of Feet

Confederate Forces
Federal Forces
Railroad
Turnpike road
The ═ ═ ═ lines mark the different positions occupied
by the Enemy, and from which they were driven.
The .... lines mark the movements of our Regiments
from one position to another.
Our forces are here represented in the four distinct positions
which they occupied, from the Road-Crossing near which the
fight opened, to where the Enemy's retrograde movement began;
from this point our whole line advanced in pursuit.

M.B. GRANT
Lieut.Corps Engrs. C.S
Del.

A map of the Battle of Olustee

Union (10 percent of the voters in the 1860 census), he could represent Florida's three electoral votes for President Lincoln in the upcoming election.[3] On February 8, Seymour's troops captured the Confederate positions at Camp Finegan and Ten Mile Run. Seymour decided to keep pushing west. He sent a letter to Gillmore detailing his plan. Shocked, Gillmore sent an officer to call the troops back. But the officer arrived too late. Events went into motion that resulted in Florida's largest battle of the war.

The Meeting at Ocean Pond

The Confederacy expected an attack, thanks to communication from General Beauregard in Charleston. On February 8, Governor Milton sent a telegram to Secretary of War Seddon asking for five thousand troops.[4] Because of their need for food, the Confederate Army could no longer afford to lose Florida. Twelve regiments of Georgia soldiers were sent to join six Florida units converging at Lake City. By February 20, there were more than five thousand Confederate soldiers prepared to fight. General Joseph Finegan, the commander of Florida's forces, chose a spot along the railroad that could be easily defended, just east of the railroad station at Olustee.

On February 20, 1864, Seymour's forces met the Confederate advance. Scouts let Finegan know of the Union approach. Finegan sent the cavalry to draw the Union forces toward his defensible position. Skirmishes in the woods soon turned into a formal battle. Soldiers lined up and marched toward each other. Private Milton M. Woodford of the 7th Connecticut Infantry stood in the front line of Union soldiers. "As we advanced," he reported, "the enemy retired, keeping just in sight. Whenever we could get near enough to stand any chance of doing execution we would blaze away at them and they returned the fire in a way that showed that they were good marksmen. . . . "[5]

The first Confederate brigade, led by General Alfred H. Colquitt, swung into action. On the Union side, the 7th New Hampshire Infantry joined in, but misunderstood their orders. Their line collapsed in confusion. Behind them, the 8th U.S. Colored Troops moved in to fill the gap. It was their first battle. Wrote officer Oliver Norton, "We were not more than two hundred yards from the enemy, concealed in pits and behind trees, and what did the regiment do? At first they were stunned, bewildered, and knew not what to do. They curled to the ground, and as men fell around them they seemed terribly scared, but gradually they recovered their senses and commenced firing." Finally, their officers ordered them to retreat. "As the men fell back they gathered in groups like frightened sheep . . . into these groups the rebels poured the deadliest fire, almost every bullet hitting some one."[6] The Confederates advanced on the retreating Union soldiers, their defensive line stretching a mile long. Three New York regiments held the line.

Brigadier General Alfred Holt Colquitt

in the center of the battle, and every fellow was straining his voice with the Rebel Yell, opening fire upon the enemy."[7] General Finegan arrived, as did a train loaded with ammunition—and fresh gunners.

"For four hours, from two o'clock until six, the battle raged, the Union troops receiving three bullets for every one they could return."[8] It was only a matter of time before they would have to quit the battlefield.

The Retreat

By late afternoon, General Seymour knew he'd lost the battle. Covering his injured soldiers, he sent in fresh troops to protect the retreat. These two black regiments, the 54th Massachusetts and the 1st North Carolina Colored Volunteers, held the line and confused the Confederates by breaking out in sporadic cheers. Behind them, the survivors of the 7th Connecticut closed the line. But darkness was falling. After four hours of battle, thousands of men lay dying. Ten thousand had met in the pine forest, the sides evenly matched. The Union lost nearly two thousand soldiers—killed, missing, and wounded. The Confederates suffered almost a thousand casualties.

Nearly running out of ammunition, the Confederates received reinforcements just in time. George Dorman recounts. "About 1 o'clock the First Florida Battalion . . . went to the rescue of General Colquitt . . . . We struck right

Officers of the 54th Massachusetts Volunteer Infantry

The Union Army retreated toward Jacksonville. At Barber's Ford, mules dragged several railroad cars filled with three hundred wounded soldiers to Baldwin. At Baldwin, soldiers burned the Confederate depot and storehouses, then hooked up a locomotive to the railroad cars. The train made it from Baldwin to Ten-Mile Station before the locomotive broke down. The 54th Massachusetts was ordered back to help. By sheer muscle power, they moved the train

Soldiers of the 54th Massachusetts Volunteer Infantry

three miles closer to Jacksonville before enough horses were rounded up to finish the task.

A Question of Honor

After each battle of the Civil War, prisoners of war were rounded up and taken away from the battlefield. They would be shipped to a prison camp or paroled—set free to make their way home. When the Union Army received a list of wounded and prisoners from the Confederate forces at Olustee, few black soldiers were listed. Since three black regiments fought in the battle, the Union officers made an assumption. "It is well known that most of the wounded colored men were murdered on the field," wrote Brigadier General John P. Hatch. "Those outrages were perpetuated, as far as I can ascertain, by the Georgia Regulars and the Georgia Volunteers of Colquitt's brigade. . . . All accounts represent the Florida troops as not engaged in the murders."[9]

One Lake City woman, Ruth, helped out in the hospital after the battle: "The Federal wounded came to us, consisting almost entirely of negroes; three regiments of these poor creatures having been made to receive our bayonets, and their mutilated bodies tell with what effect. . . . "[10] A large body of evidence suggests that black prisoners were treated inhumanely in the aftermath of the battle.

The Aftermath

John Hay returned to Washington embarrassed. The *New York Herald* tied his expedition to the Union's defeat at Olustee—"Price of Three Votes for the Presidency! One Thousand Lives!"—and published the details of correspondence between Lincoln, Hay, Gillmore, and Seymour.[11]

"The expedition in Florida, from which we expected to hear such good results, has, so far, proved a failure; in other words, our troops have been badly whipped," wrote one Union soldier to the *Boston Journal*. "Every one at his post feels sadly enough. I have seen several of the wounded today, and I feel that the whole of Florida is not worth half the suffering and anguish this battle has caused."[12]

Their victory at Olustee rallied the Confederates in Florida. General Finegan became a hero "second to no General in the army."[13] Even General Beauregard was lavish in his praise: "Your country will be cheered by this timely success, and I trust it is but the earnest of heavier and crushing blows which shall destroy our enemy on the soil of Florida."[14]

Chapter 11

Florida's Final Stand

By March 1865, Florida had been nibbled around the edges by Union occupation. Jacksonville, St. Augustine, Pensacola, Tampa, and Key West all lay firmly under Union control. Yet the state capital, Tallahassee, remained free. When word spread that Tallahassee might be invaded, the 1st Florida Reserves caught a train to assume positions to the south of the city. S.M. Hankins describes the ride:

"Everything went well until just as day began to dawn. We were going down grade and around a curve. The Engineer called for Brake, with a loud whistle from the locomotive. Then he began to blow distress whistle as fast as he could." Down ahead, he could see the railroad trestle was on fire! "There was not enough brakes to check his speed. He found he could not stop, so he put on all the power his engine had, and landed us all O.K. across a burning bridge on the Aucilla River! Some of the bridge fell in as the last car got off of it."[1]

Union soldiers were slipping toward Tallahassee. They'd employed local Confederate deserters to burn the bridge. Confederate and Union forces would clash in Florida's final battle of the war.

The Battle of Natural Bridge

Predicting that most of Florida's troops were sent to attack Fort Myers, Union Brigadier General John Newton, the commander of the District of Key West and Tortugas, believed the time was right to invade Tallahassee. On March 4, 1865, more than a thousand Union soldiers landed at St. Marks. The limited forces of the

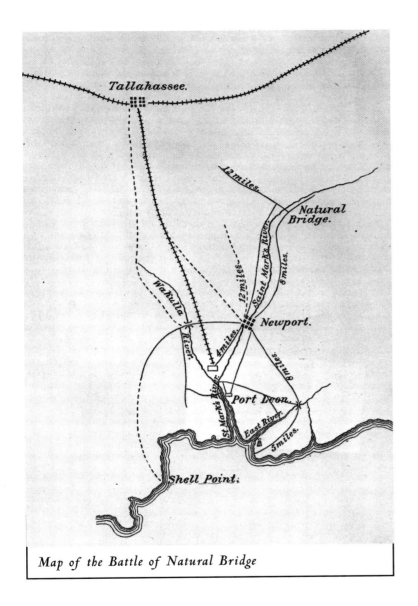

Map of the Battle of Natural Bridge

5th Florida Cavalry under Lieutenant Colonel George W. Scott faced the Union troops. Wrote Scott, "I . . . threw my command in front & flanks of the enemy and harassed him as much as possible in his march on Newport. . . . finding they were moving towards the Natural bridge I immediately marched to that place and took position commanding the crossing."[2]

By March 6, the Union troops reached the Natural Bridge, a place where the St. Marks River flows underground for a short distance. Militia and cadets from the Florida Military Institute in Tallahassee (known as the West Florida Seminary at the outset of the war) joined the regular troops to meet the enemy. Cadet Charles Beard recounts, "The fighting in front of us in the river hammock was fast & furious. Scott & his gallant men were giving a good account of the enemy & held their ground till about 11 o'clock, I think, when of a sudden was heard a terrible yell! & the 2nd Fla. Cavalry was in it. The musketing rather became a roar & for an hour perhaps it kept up—then the enemy found it was a bigger bite that he could masticate & gave way making as fast time as possible. Where we were was directly in line of the fire & the bullets

Federals had fallen back to the outside of the swamp on the road and had begun to throw up breastworks . . . . It was getting late in the afternoon when we heard an insistent roar of small arms across the swamp. We knew that our men had successfully crossed, but the result of the firing we did not know. We had not long to wait. A courier from the commander came and notified us that our men had come up in the rear of the Federal breastwork and after emptying their guns, the Federal troops had fled in disorder, leaving their dead in our hands."[4]

As the Union troops retreated, the Confederates followed them. "The fighting was still pretty heavy," recounted Cadet Beard, "tho the enemy was retreating, when we were ordered to march back to Newport in order to meet them in case they made an attempt to cross."[5] The cadets had their first meal in a day. "We had rations of corn pone served to us—no meat, no drink save river water—we had not campaigned long enough to create an appetite for corn pone so it was used for ammunition in a bread battle!"[6]

With the Confederate victory at Natural Bridge, Tallahassee remained free for the remainder of the war. But the war was ending on distant fronts.

cut the trees & knocked the dust up from our extempor breastworks above & around us."[3]

Meanwhile, another Florida unit managed a sneak attack. According to James Dancy, "Some of our soldiers, native, knew of a foot-log below the Natural Bridge. The

The Florida Assassin

A little-known story about President Lincoln's assassination involves a young man from Jasper, Florida. Lewis Powell enlisted in the 2nd Florida Infantry. Wounded at Gettysburg, he was taken prisoner but escaped, making his way back to the front lines. Sent to join the Confederate Secret Service, Powell—alias Lewis Payne—worked with John Wilkes Booth, John Surratt, and others to plot the assassination of President Lincoln. In the same hour that Lincoln was shot, "Payne" attempted to kill Secretary of State William H. Seward. For his role in the plot, Powell received the death penalty.

Lewis Payne, conspirator in Abraham Lincoln's assassination

Never Surrender

Governor Milton worked tirelessly to ensure Florida's safety. But he sensed the collapse of the Confederacy. All along he was adamant about his support for the cause. "Death would be preferable to reunion," he told the Florida legislature in November 1864.[7] On April 1, 1865, eight days before General Lee surrendered, Milton returned home to his plantation in Marianna and shot himself. It would be up to his successor to tender Florida's surrender and await the Union Army's arrival in Tallahassee.

For the rest of Florida, the war ended less dramatically. Men who heard the news of the surrender headed home. But prison still loomed for some. Fleeing south from Richmond, Stephen Mallory met up with his family in LaGrange, Georgia, on May 20, 1865. He was arrested in the middle of the night and taken to Fort Lafayette, where he spent ten months in prison. After his release in March 1866, he rejoined his family in Pensacola and resumed his law practice.

David Yulee would also be arrested, but not just for his treasonous letter. Yulee was one of several Floridians who helped high-ranking members of the Confederate government escape the country.

Flight through Florida

After the fall of Richmond, President Jefferson Davis and his cabinet fled south. Several of the men thought it possible to escape via Florida to the Trans-Mississippi Department, where General Edmund Kirby-Smith didn't even know the war was over. Davis and his cabinet risked being hanged for treason. Leaving the country was the only good solution, and Florida the only safe route.

Along with Mallory, President Jefferson Davis was captured in Georgia. But his baggage, traveling with several of his officers, ended up at David Yulee's plantation in Archer on the evening of May 22. Yulee hid the luggage in a storeroom, but a coachman turned him in. Union troops came to seize it. On May 25, Yulee was arrested in Gainesville, then set free. But on June 18, the federal authorities sent him to Fort Pulaski "for safekeeping."[8] Although threatened with the death sentence for his letter, he was finally released on March 25, 1866.

Secretary of War General John C. Breckenridge arrived in Gainesville on May 22. He asked Captain J. J. Dickison for help. "The only means of transportation that I could offer was a lifeboat I had captured with the gunboat *Columbine* on the St. Johns river. This I had secured by sinking it in a lake."[10] They retrieved the boat and brought it to Silver Springs. Breckenridge and two of Dickison's men rowed up the St. Johns, had the boat carried to Indian River, and slipped past the blockade, successfully sailing to the Bahamas.

Secretary of State Judah Benjamin disguised himself as a French journalist, "M. Bonfal." Reaching Brooksville in late May, he enlisted the confidence of Captain LeRoy Lesley, who escorted him to the Gamble Plantation on the Manatee River. Benjamin enjoyed comfortable surroundings with his host, Captain Archibald McNeil. McNeil arranged a boat from Sarasota to Nassau, allowing Benjamin to escape.

Attorney General George Davis made slow progress, arriving in New Smyrna in September. He chartered a boat to Nassau. It was hurricane season, and the boat couldn't handle the rough seas. The captain sailed down the coast to Key West, where Davis hoped to hire a boat to Cuba. The federal authorities discovered him, arresting him in November.

Reunited Once More

On May 10, 1865, the Union Army marched into Tallahassee and took control of the government from Acting Governor Abraham K. Allison. Florida formally rejoined the United States of America.

The federal government spread the word about the end of slavery. General McCook posted an order "reminding" Floridians of the Emancipation Proclamation.

Wrote Ellen Call Long, daughter of ex-Governor Richard Call, "There was a broad grin on every countenance; shaking of hands, and a general air of extreme satisfaction, but no outbreaks, no offensiveness; nothing to indicate a feeling of triumph, or joy of escape from thraldrom. Some families were disturbed by the sudden departure of house servants, but generally both white and black accepted the situation together, willing to wait and learn the duty required respectively."[10]

Florida's soldiers returned from distant battlefields and settled back to their farms and plantations. Although the battle scars would remain, most Floridians were simply glad that the war was over.

Source Notes

Abbreviations: ORA = *Official Records (Army)*. ORN = *Official Records (Navy)*. PHRC = Lelia Abercrombie Library, Pensacola Historical Society Research Center. P.K. Yonge = University of Florida Special Collections, P.K. Yonge Library of Florida History. SAHS = St. Augustine Historical Society Library. UF = University of Florida. USF = Special Collections, University of South Florida Library.

Preface

1. John Milton, Letter to Jefferson Davis, October 29, 1861. Governor's Office Letterbooks 1836–1909, Volume 6, Florida State Archives.
2. J. J. Dickison, *Military History of Florida* (Atlanta: Confederate Publishing Company, 1899), p. 138.

Chapter 1

1. Frances Smith, Letter to Edmund Kirby-Smith, January 16, 1861. Kirby-Smith Papers, Roll 2, SAHS.
2. Smith, January 16, 1861.
3. Smith, January 16, 1861.
4. John F. Reiger, "Antiwar and Pro-Union Sentiment in Confederate Florida" (Master's thesis, UF, 1966), p. 14.
5. Madison S. Perry, Letter to the President and Delegates of the Convention of the Independent State of South Carolina, December 24, 1860. Letters, 1860–1862, P.K. Yonge.
6. Richard Keith Call, Letter to Mr. Hart, Editor, *Tallahassee Sentinel*, December 22, 1860. Call Family Papers, Florida State Archives.
7. Ellen Call Long, "Florida Breezes," p. 230. P.K. Yonge.
8. "Gen. Edmund Kirby Smith," *Florida Times-Union*, May 30, 1965.
9. James Raab. *W. W. Loring: Florida's Forgotten General* (Shawnee Mission, Kansas: Sunflower University Press, 1996), pp. 34–35.
10. Philip Thomas Tucker, *Civil War Chronicles: From Auction Block to Glory: the African-American Experience* (New York: Metrobooks, 1998), pp. 72–79.

Chapter 2

1. Virginia Parks, Alan Rick, and Norman Simons, *Pensacola in The Civil War* (Pensacola: Pensacola Historical Society, 1978), p. 11.
2. J. Thomas Scharf, *History of the Confederate States Navy* (New York: Rogers & Sherwood, 1887). Mallory biography file, PHRC.
3. "A Plan to Avoid Civil War," *The Annals of America* (Chicago: Encyclopædia Britannica, 1968), Volume 9, p. 256.
4. John S.C. Abbott, "Florida, Her Crime and Punishment," *Harper's New Monthly Magazine*, Vol. 33, Issue 198, November 1866, p. 705.
5. Loomis Langdon, Letter, April 16, 1861. Papers, 1856–1906, Box 2. Florida State Archives.
6. Parks, p. 15.
7. Len M. Griffin, Letter to father, April 3, 1861, P.K. Yonge.
8. Joseph Dill Alison, Diary entry, July 12, 1861, P.K. Yonge.
9. Abbott, p. 707.
10. Roderick Gospero Shaw, Letter to sister, October 9, 1861, Florida State Archives.
11. David P. Ogden, *The Fort Barrancas Story* (Eastern National), p. 20.
12. Judy Taylor, "Government in Exile," *Quarterly Publication, Butler County Historical Society*, Volume 27, No. 2, April 1991.
13. W.H. Judah, March 28, 1864, Document of military exemption. McKeller file, Box 1 Folder 2, PHRC.
14. Francis W. Bobe, Letter to W.H. Judah, March 30, 1865. McKeller file, Box 1 Folder 2, PHRC.
15. J.H. Alexander, Receipt, July 3 1865 to Filo de La Rua. McKeller file, Box 1 Folder 2, PHRC.

Chapter 3

1. John Appleyard, *Stephen R. Mallory, Secretary of the Navy, Confederate States of America* (Pensacola: John Appleyard Agency, 1993), p. 13.
2. Rodney Dillon, Jr., "The Civil War in South Florida" (Master's thesis, UF, 1980), p. 195.
3. Robert Watson, Diary entry, September 27, 1861. Diary, 1861–1865, Florida State Archives.
4. Letters Sent by the Department of Florida, Letter from Commander of Fort Pickens to Commander of Fort Taylor, May 2, 1861. April 1861–January 1869, SAHS.
5. ORA Series I, Volume I, p. 430.
6. Christian Boye, Letter to son, September 23, 1861, P.K. Yonge.
7. Dillon, p. 195.
8. Louis James M. Boyd, Letter to wife, August 17, 1862. "Letters, 1861–1871: Naval Operations Aboard the Albatross," P.K. Yonge.
9. Walter Keeler Scofield, June 22, 1863. "Journal Aboard the USS *Sagamore*, Nov 23 1861 through Apr 9 1864," P.K. Yonge.
10. Scofield, April 21, 1862.
11. Scofield, April 29, 1862.
12. Boyd, Letter to wife, November 27, 1862.
13. Robert Taylor, "Rebel Beef: Florida Cattle & the Confederacy, 1861–1865" (Master's thesis, UF, 1985), p. 35.

Chapter 4

1. Mills M. Lord, "David Levy Yulee, Statesman and Railroad Builder" (Master's thesis, UF, 1940), pp. 153-154.
2. J. J. Dickison, *Military History of Florida* (Atlanta: Confederate Publishing Company, 1899), p. 21.
3. Karl A. Bickel, "Robert E. Lee in Florida," *Florida Historical Quarterly*, Volume 27, July 1948.
4. G. H. Dorman, *Fifty Years Ago: Reminiscences of 1861–65* (Tallahassee: T. J. Appleyard), p. 3.
5. ORA Series I, Volume XLVII, Part II, p. 1390.
6. Lord, pp. 154–156.
7. John Milton, Letter to David Yulee, June 8, 1863, USF.

Chapter 5

1. John Milton, Letter to Jefferson Davis, October 29, 1861, Florida State Archives.
2. Joseph Dill Alison, Diary entry, May 9, 1861, P. K. Yonge.
3. Alison, June 11, 1861.
4. Robert Watson, Diary entry, January 6, 1862. Florida State Archives.
5. Milton to Stephen Mallory, November 2, 1861, Florida State Archives.
6. Washington Waters, Letter, May 11, 1864, P. K. Yonge.
7. Officers of the 1st FL Cavalry to Milton, March 14th 1862, Florida State Archives.

8. Jim R. Cabaniss, "Civil War Journal and Letters of Washington Ives, 4th FL CSA," 1987, P. K. Yonge.
9. Joseph H. Crute, Jr., *Units of the Confederate States Army* (Gaithersburg, MD: Olde Soldier Books, Inc., 1987 reprint).
10. Cabaniss.
11. A. J. Neal, Letter, February 14, 1864. Letters of 1st Lt. A. J. Neal, Marion Light Artillery CSA, Museum of Southern History, Jacksonville.
12. Frances Smith, Letter to son, December 2, 1861, Kirby-Smith Papers, Roll 2, SAHS.
13. Catherine Hopley, *Life in the South by a Blockaded British Subject* (London: William Clowes & Sons, 1863), pp. 276–277.
14. A. J. Neal, March 24, 1864.
15. Robert Taylor, "Rebel Beef: Florida Cattle & the Confederacy, 1861–1865" (Master's thesis, UF, 1985), p. 112.
16. William Ellison, Letter, March 26, 1863, USF.
17. Sallie Mickler, Letter to Capt. Jacob E. Mickler, June 3, 1862, Pizzo Collection, USF.

Chapter 6

1. J. J. Dickison, *Military History of Florida* (Atlanta: Confederate Publishing Company, 1899), pp. 24–25.
2. W. C. Middleton, Diary. SAHS.
3. John S. C. Abbott, "Florida, Her Crime and Punishment," *Harper's New Monthly Magazine*, Volume 33, Issue 198, November 1866, p. 710.

4. Frances Smith, Letter to son, March 12, 1862. Kirby-Smith Papers, Roll 2, SAHS.

5. Thomas Graham, *The Awakening of St. Augustine* (St. Augustine: St. Augustine Historical Society, 1978) p. 88.

6. "A Story of the War. Only Three Women Knew It—Why Mrs. Smith was ordered beyond the Union Line," *St. Augustine Evening Record*, January 5, 1895.

7. Blakley Mason, Letter, April 24, 1863, SAHS.

8. George Colt, Letter, November 11, 1862, Pizzo Collection, USF.

9. Sam Proctor, "Jacksonville During the Civil War," *Florida Historical Quarterly*, Volume 41, April 1963.

10. John Drysdale II, Letter, March 20, 1862, Biography file, SAHS.

11. Thomas Wentworth Higginson, *Army Life in a Black Regiment* (Boston: Fields, Osgood, & Co. 1870), p. 118.

12. Higginson, pp. 108–109.

Chapter 7

1. Milton F. Perry, *Infernal Machines: The Story of Confederate Submarine and Mine Warfare* (Baton Rouge: Louisiana State University Press, 1965), pp. 114–115.

2. John Milton, Letter received March 25, 1862, Florida State Archives.

3. Maxine Turner, *Navy Gray: A Story of the Confederate Navy on the Chattahoochee and Apalachicola Rivers* (Tuscaloosa: University of Alabama Press, 1988), pp. 187–188.

4. Walter Keeler Scofield, June 6, 1862. "Journal Aboard the USS *Sagamore*, Nov 23 1861 through Apr 9 1864," P. K. Yonge.

5. Turner, pp. 190–191.

6. James M. Dancy, "Memoirs of the Civil War and Reconstruction," September 1, 1933, P. K. Yonge.

7. Mary Elizabeth Dickison, *Dickison and His Men* (Gainesville: University of Florida Press, 1962 reprint), pp. 62–68.

8. J. J. Dickison, *Military History of Florida* (Atlanta: Confederate Publishing Company, 1899), pp. 84–85.

Chapter 8

1. ORN Series I, Volume XXV, Part II, pp. 737–738.

2. ORN Series I, Volume XIII, p. 369.

3. James M. Dancy, "Memoirs of the Civil War and Reconstruction," September 1, 1933, P. K. Yonge.

4. Frank Howard, "Wakulla County—Some Civil War Action," *Wakulla Area Digest*, April 1994.

5. Walter Keeler Scofield, Diary entry, September 11, 1862.

6. Charles Carroll Fishburne, Jr., *The Cedar Keys in the 19th Century* (Cedar Key: Cedar Key Historical Society, 1997), p. 57.

7. Robert Taylor, "Rebel Beef: Florida Cattle & the Confederacy, 1861–1865" (Master's thesis, UF, 1985), p. 21.

8. Mills M. Lord, "David Levy Yulee, Statesman and Railroad Builder" (Master's thesis, UF, 1940), p. 156.

9. Rodney Dillon, Jr., "The Civil War in South Florida" (Master's thesis, UF, 1980), p. 207.

10. Taylor, p. 26.
11. Dillon, pp. 131–141.
12. ORA Series I, Volume XXVIII, Part II, p. 472.
13. ORA Series I, Volume XXVIII, Part II, p. 473.
14. James McKay, Sr., Letter to Pleasants Woodson White, February 4, 1864, USF.
15. Dillon, pp. 290–291.
16. Thomas Ellis, "Personal account of service in the war," Florida State Archives.
17. Thomas Wentworth Higginson, *Army Life in a Black Regiment.* (Boston: Fields, Osgood, & Co. 1870), p. 422.

Chapter 9

1. Jerrell H. Shofner, *Jackson County, Florida—A History* (The Jackson County Heritage Association, 1985), p. 239.
2. Robert Watson, Diary entry, September 23, 1863. Florida State Archives.
3. John F. Reiger, *Antiwar and Pro-Union Sentiment in Confederate Florida* (Master's thesis, UF, 1966), p. 67.
4. Reiger, p. 68.
5. Jim R. Cabaniss, Civil War Journal and Letters of Washington Ives, 4th FL CSA, Transcription, 1987, P. K. Yonge.
6. Reiger, p. 87.

7. Rodney Dillon, Jr., "The Civil War in South Florida" (Master's thesis, UF, 1980), p. 249–250.
8. Joel Watkins, Letter from sister, SAHS.
9. James McKay, Sr., Letter to Pleasants Woodson White, May 3, 1864, USF.
10. Dillon, p. 262.
11. George Colt, Letter, November 11, 1862. Pizzo Collection, USF.
12. S. M. Hankins, "My Recollections of the Confederate War," p. 18. Florida State Archives.
13. William H. Nulty, *Confederate Florida: The Road to Olustee* (Tuscaloosa: University of Alabama Press, 1990), p. 55.
14. ORA Series I, Volume XXVI, Part I, p. 874.
15. Mark Curenton, *Tories & Deserters—the 1st Florida Cavalry* (1988), p. 26.
16. Dale Cox, *The West Florida War* (Bascom, Florida: Jackson Publications, 1989).
17. "Eyewitness Tells of Burning of Church," *The Kalendar*, St. Lukes Episcopal Church, Marianna. June 1, 1931, P. K. Yonge.

Chapter 10

1. Winston Stephens, Letter to wife, February 21, 1864. Winston-Octavia Stephens Papers, P. K. Yonge.
2. ORA Series I, Volume XXXV, Part I, p. 279.

3. Carl Sandburg, *Abraham Lincoln: The Prairie Years and the War Years* (New York: Harcourt Brace Jovanovich, 1954), p. 497.

4. John Milton, Letter to James A. Seddon, February 10, 1864, USF.

5. Vaughn D. Bornet, "A Connecticut Yankee Fights at Olustee," *Florida Historical Quarterly*, Volume 27, October 1948.

6. Lewis G. Schmidt, *The Civil War In Florida: A Military History. Volume II, The Battle of Olustee.* (Allentown: Lewis G. Schmidt, 1989), p. 217.

7. George H. Dorman, *Fifty Years Ago: Reminiscences of '61-65* (Tallahassee: T. J. Appleyard).

8. John S.C. Abbott, "Florida, Her Crime and Punishment," *Harper's New Monthly Magazine*, Vol. 33, Issue 198, November 1866, p. 718.

9. ORA Series II, Volume VII, p. 876.

10. Ellen Call Long, "Florida Breezes," p. 273, P. K. Yonge.

11. Sandburg, p. 498.

12. *Boston Journal*, February 29, 1864.

13. Schmidt, p. 370.

14. ORA Series I, Volume XXXV, Part I, p. 338

Chapter 11

1. S.M. Hankins, "My Recollections of the Confederate War," p. 28. Florida State Archives.

2. George Washington Scott, Letter, March 10, 1865. Papers 1850–1904, Florida State Archives.

3. Charles W. Beard, Letter to Francis P. Fleming, August 7, 1905, P. K. Yonge.

4. James M. Dancy, "Memoirs of the Civil War and Reconstruction," September 1, 1933, P. K. Yonge.

5. Beard, August 7, 1905.

6. Beard, August 7, 1905.

7. Rodney Dillon, Jr., "The Civil War in South Florida" (Master's thesis, UF, 1980), p. 318.

8. Mills M. Lord, "David Levy Yulee, Statesman and Railroad Builder," (Master's thesis, UF, 1940), pp. 169–178.

9. Mary Elizabeth Dickison, *Dickison and His Men* (Gainesville: University of Florida Press, 1962 reprint), pp. 224–227.

10. Ellen Call Long, "Florida Breezes," pp. 284–285, P. K. Yonge.

Recommended Resources

Further Reading

Black, Wallace B. and Jean F. Blashfield. *Blockade Runners and Ironclads: Naval Action in the Civil War*. Danbury, Connecticut: Franklin Watts, 1997.

Blakey, Arch Fredric, Ann S. Lainhart, and Winston Bryant Stephens Jr., editors. *Rose Cottage Chronicles: Civil War Letters of the Bryant-Stephens Families of North Florida*. Gainesville: University Press of Florida, 1998.

Clark, James C. *Last Train South: The Flight of the Confederate Government from Richmond*. Jackson, Mississippi: McFarland & Company, 1997.

Loderhouse, Gary. *Far, Far From Home: The Ninth Florida Regiment in the Confederate Army*. Indiana: Guild Press of Indiana, 1999.

Murphy, Jim. *The Boys' War: Confederate and Union Soldiers Talk About the Civil War*. New York: Clarion Books, 1990.

Nulty, William H. *Confederate Florida: The Road to Olustee*. Alabama: University of Alabama Press, 1990.

Owensby, Betty. *"Alias Paine"—Lewis Thortnton Powell, the Mystery Man of the Lincoln Conspiracy*. Jefferson, North Carolina: McFarland Press, 1993.

Raab, James. *W. W. Loring: Florida's Forgotten General*. Shawnee Mission, Kansas: Sunflower University Press, 1999.

On the World Wide Web

Try keywords like "Civil War" or "Confederacy" with "Florida" in your favorite search engine to come up with sites pertaining to the topic.

The Battle of Olustee

http://extlab1.entnem.ufl.edu/olustee/

Extensive Web site at the University of Florida covering the Battle of Olustee, including full text of newspaper articles about the battle and letters from participants.

The Civil War in Florida
http://dhr.dos.state.fl.us/museum/civwar/
Presentation mirroring the large Civil War exhibit at the Florida State Museum. From the Florida State Archives.

The Civil War in Florida: Letters of a New Hampshire Soldier
http://www.library.miami.edu/archives/shedd/index.htm
Transcribed letters of a member of the Union Army, plus photos and detailed background information on his stay in Florida. From the University of Miami.

Maple Leaf Shipwreck: An Extraordinary American Civil War Shipwreck
http://www.mapleleafshipwreck.com/
In-depth details on the wreck of the *Maple Leaf* and the underwater archeological work done to bring artifacts to the surface.

Up the St. Marys
http://web.uflib.ufl.edu/spec/pkyonge/armylife.html
A scanned chapter from the Thomas Wentworth Higgins biography *Army Life in a Black Regiment*, published in 1870, detailing the service of black Union soliders under his command. Presented by the P.K. Yonge Library of Florida History.

The William Wing Loring World Wide Web site
http://home.earthlink.net/~atomic_rom/loring.htm
Extensive biographical information about this flamboyant Floridian who commanded Confederate forces under Robert E. Lee and Stonewall Jackson. Created by Civil War history buff Michael Butzgy.

Places to Visit

Providing great background on Florida during the Civil War, numerous parks offer interpretive tours or exhibits. Don't miss Olustee Battlefield (Olustee), Natural Bridge Battlefield (Woodville), the Gamble Plantation (Ellenton), and the Yulee Sugar Mill Ruins (Homosassa). The Union Blockading Squadron based ships out of Egmont Key (St. Petersburg), now a state park. Remains of Civil War riverside earthen battlements exist in Torreya State Park (Bristol) and Suwannee River State Park (Live Oak). Cattle drives stopped in the Paynes Prairie State Reserve (Gainesville) on their way to Georgia. At Lake Kissimmee State Park (Lake Wales), an 1870s cow camp sets up every weekend.

Florida's major forts all played a significant role in the war. All are open to the public. You can visit Fort Pickens and Fort Barrancas in Pensacola, Fort Clinch in Fernandina Beach, Castillo de San Marcos (Fort Marion) in St. Augustine, Fort Taylor on Key West, and Fort Jefferson in the Dry Tortugas. These forts and many other sites around the state host living history presentations—Union and Confederate garrisons, and annual reenactments of battles. The Battle of Olustee (third weekend of February) is one of the largest Civil War reenactments in the southeastern United States, drawing five thousand or more participants each year. Check the Battle of Olustee Web site for a calendar of reenactments throughout Florida.

Several museums in the state focus on the Civil War with special exhibits. The Civil War Soldiers Museum in Pensacola gives an overview of the war, with special emphasis on Pensacola and military medicine. The Museum of Florida History in Tallahassee has an extensive Civil War exhibit. Excavated remains from the *Maple Leaf* are on display at the Museum of Science and Industry in Jacksonville, and the Museum of Southern History in Jacksonville has general exhibits and a large library. In St. Augustine, the Museum of Weapons & Early American History shows off Civil War artifacts. A giant iron salt kettle sits outside the Cedar Key State Museum, which covers the region's role in the war. Lighthouse tours and museums spotlight Civil War history at Jupiter Inlet, Key Biscayne, Key West, Pensacola, Ponce Inlet, St. Augustine, and St. Marks.

Index

Page numbers in *italics* refer to illustrations.

Alison, Joseph Dill, 32
Allison, Abraham K., 69
Amelia Island, 27, 28
Apalachicola River, 43

Bailey, Theodorus, 24
Baldwin, Florida, 30, 31
Beard, Charles, 65, 66
Beauregard, Pierre G.T., 46, 60, 63
Benjamin, Judah, 69
Blacks, 9, 12, 35–36, 39, 41, *54*, 55, *56*, 61–63, *62*, 69
Blockade runners, 22, 26, 35, 37, 40, 50
Booth, John Wilkes, 67
Boyd, Louis, 24, 25
Boye, Christian, 24
Bragg, Braxton, 18, 19, 21, 35
Brannan, John M., 22
Breckenridge, John C., 69
Brooklyn (sloop of war), 16–18

Brown, Harvey, 24
Bryan, E. Pliny, 46–47
Buchanan, James, 17

Call, Richard Keith, 12, 13
Cattle, 48, 50–52, *51*
Chase, Wiliam, 16, 18
Chattahoochee River, 43
Chattanooga, Battle of, 35
Colombine (steamer), 45–46, *46*
Colquitt, Alfred Holt, 60–61, *61*
Colt, George, 39, 55
Crops, 49–50

Dancy, James, 66
Davis, George, 69
Davis, Jefferson, 9, 19, 22, 68
Deserters, 54–55, 57
Dickison, John Jackson, 10, 45, *45*, 69
Diseases, 24

Dorman, George, 28, 61
Drysdale, John, II, 40

Ellis, Thomas, 52
Ellison, William, 36

Ferguson, John "Alligator" Justice, *33*
Fernandina, Florida, 27, 28, *29*, 30, 31
5th Florida Cavalry, 65
54th Massachusetts Volunteer Infantry, 61, 62, *62*
Finegan, Joseph, 27, 60, 61, 63
1st Florida Cavalry, 34
1st Florida Infantry, 13
Fort Barrancas, 16, *18*, 18
Fort Clinch, 12, 28, 30
Fort Jefferson, 22–24
Fort Marion, 12, *38*
Fort McRee, 18, *19*, 21
Fort Pickens, 16–21

Fort Sumter, 16–18
Fort Taylor, 22–23, *23*

Gillmore, Quincy, 58, 59, 63
Grant, Ulysses S., 50
Grey, Horace, 25
Griffin, Len, 19
Guerin, H.C., 52

Hankins, S.M., 64
Harper, Mary, 35
Hay, John, 58, 63
Higginson, Thomas Wentworth, 41, 50
Hopley, Catherine, 35

Ives, Washington, 35, 54

Jacksonville, Florida, 30, 39–41, *40*, 64
Jones, Samuel, 21
Judah (police schooner), 19

Key West, Florida, 17, 22–24, 37, 64
Kirby-Smith, Edmund, 13–14, *14*, 39, 68

Langdon, Loomis, 18–19
Lee, Robert E., 14, 28, 33, 68
Lincoln, Abraham, 10, 17, 58, 59, 63, 67
Long, Ellen Call, 69
Loring, William Wing, 14–15

Mallory, Stephen R., 12, 13, 15, 16–17, 22, 32, 68
Mandarin Point, 46, 47
Maple Leaf (steamer), 47
Marianna, Florida, 57

Mason, Blakley, 39
McKay, James, 50, 52, 55
Meigs, Montgomery C., 23
Mickler, Sallie, 36
Milton, John, 9–10, 26, 30–32, *32*, 37, 42–43, 53, 55, 60, 68

Natural Bridge, Battle of, 64–66, *65*
Naval stores, 50
Neal, A.J., 35
Newton, John, 64
Northrup, Lucius B., 52
Norton, Oliver, 60

Olustee, Battle of, 58–63, *59*

Parket, Walter Miles, *34*
Pearson, J.W., 51
Pensacola, Florida, 16–19, *17*, 21, 64
Pensacola Navy Yard, 12, 18, 21
Perry, Madison Starke, 11–12, *13*
Philips, Ethelred, 54
Plantations, *49*, 49–50
Powell, Lewis (Lewis Payne), *67*, 67

Railroads, 27, 28, 30–31, *31*
Richards, John R., 53
Rogers, C.R.P., 37

St. Augustine, Florida, 9, 11, 37, 39, 64
St. Johns River, 42, 43, *44*, 45–47, 69
Saltworks, 25, *26*, 48–49
Santa Rosa Island, 16, 18–21
Scofield, Walter, 24, 43
Scott, George W., 65, *66*

Secession, 9, 12–13, *13*
2nd Florida Cavalry, 45, 65
Seward, William H., 17, 67
Seymour, Truman A., 41, 58–61, 63
Shaw, Roderick, 20
6th New York Infantry, *20*, 20–21
Slaves, 9, 12, 35–36, 55
Slemmer, Adam J., 16, 17
Smith, Frances, 11, 35, 39
Spies, 35
Stephens, Winston, 58
Summerlin, Jacob "King of the Crackers," 51
Surratt, John, 67

Tallahassee, Florida, 9, 10, 64, 66, 69
Tampa, Florida, 51, 64
Torpedoes, 42–43, 46–47
Trapier, James H., 27, 28, 30, 37

Union blockade, 22, 24–26, 35, 37, 50

Viper (armored boat), 43

Wall, P.G., 54
Waters, Washington, 34
Watkins, Joel, 55
Watson, Robert, 23–24, 32, 53
Women, 35
Woodbury, Daniel P., 55
Woodford, Milton M., 60
Woodhull, Maxwell, 48

Yulee, David L., 12–14, 27, *28*, 28, 30, 49, 50, 68